THE HOMELAND
Of The
STRONG

Kurt Eggers

INVISIBLE EMPIRE
PUBLISHING

Trigger/Offensive Content Warning and General Disclaimer:

"The law is that power which governs over life and death, over creation, decay, and rebirth, whose origin lies beyond human perception, yet whose harmony is the ultimate longing of those who know."

CONTENTS

PREFACE

Homeland of the Strong is Kurt Eggers' uncompromising call to a people's strength, discipline, and devotion to their homeland. Written with fire and conviction, it tears through illusions of comfort and materialism, demanding steadfastness, sacrifice, and unity. Eggers does not merely describe an ideal — he forges one in words, setting before his readers a vision of the homeland as sacred ground, where blood, culture, and destiny are bound together.

This work belongs to a decisive moment in Germany's history, reflecting a spirit that sought purity, resilience, and the triumph of communal life over selfishness. Eggers' prose carries the weight of myth and the sharpness of command: poetic exaltation fused with martial clarity, bound to the eternal themes of fate, strength, and loyalty to the land.

In this English edition, every effort has been made to preserve Eggers' raw intensity and unflinching tone. Nothing is softened, nothing diluted. The power of his language remains intact, so that readers encounter his vision as it was meant to be experienced — direct, unyielding, and alive.

To read **Homeland of the Strong** is to confront a philosophy that demands reflection, and perhaps resistance, but never indifference. Eggers wrote to inspire men to rise above weakness, and the echo of his words endures.

FORWARD

When I followed up my book 'On Courageous Living and Brave Dying' with the volume 'The Birth of the Millennium,' I expressed the hope that, in the not too distant future, I would be able to write a third volume about the homeland of the strong.

This third volume is now before you.

I hope that the three volumes, which in content and structure form a living unity, will be read in the sequence in which they were created.

I thank my friends in Germany and in the entire Germanic sphere for their affirmative response, which has made this volume my duty.

May 'The Homeland of the Strong' also contribute to deepening the understanding for the tremendous time in which we live, hope, and are allowed to work.

The Germanic Reich of the German nation has become a reality. Its law will continue to act until the perfect homeland of the strong is created on this earth.

To the new era, the new people!

This shall be the rallying cry of this book, which is not addressed to those of yesterday or to those beyond, but solely to those whose hearts beat for Germany and who believe in Germany, in its law, in its yearning, and in its reality!

Dortmund, April 10, 1938.

Kurt Eggers

CHAPTER

1

ON CHILDHOOD
& LONGING

In the twilight of the evening, nearly every human life brings forth — beautifying, glorifying, reassuring — the last sunbeam of memory.

There are old men and elderly women who cannot behold a carefree playing child without being deeply moved.

There are also notorious criminal natures who, in fanatical zeal, strive to come into contact with a child, seeking to be 'enchanted' by its purity.

For example, the calculating and calculated effect of numerous images of the 'Child Jesus,' who rests gently and smiling in the manger of the stable in Jewish Bethlehem, radiates especially to 'hardened' hearts.

Perhaps even today more souls are won for Christian teachings through the 'Child Jesus' than by the judging, threatening, and avenging Lord Jesus Christ.

For the already perceptive youth, the state of childhood is by no means the fulfillment of existence. On the contrary, every boy, driven to action, longs to grow into a young man and desires to overcome the state of immaturity through the deeds of young manhood. For people whose life course has been marked, childhood means a sweet lack of responsibility, a state of innocence and security, since they do not yet know the dangers of duty. For those shipwrecked by life, the mirror of self-recognition is occasionally held up, and they recognize, full of terror, that they have lost those carefree days of human existence and must shine through. The realization of having to lead a wasted life fosters the wish to once again be a child, to start life anew from the beginning, to avoid all cliffs and reefs, and, ultimately — purified by the experiences of the first and fleeting life — to successfully steer the ship of life into the harbor of security, to finally anchor in the roadstead of bliss.

In sentimental songs, whose effect becomes increasingly potent in the twilight, the sorrow for the lost paradise of childhood is given full expression. The songs of the lost 'youth time' have become national hymns for the shipwrecked of life, celebrated without the slightest trace of irony over the tear-filled hours of sentimental memories.

In contrast to the 'innocent' child stands guilt-laden humanity, which is inclined to sing a psalm of sorrow at every cradle.

Childhood!

Usually unconsciously, an ideal of life develops from a stage of growth that must be overcome and survived. The childish life of becoming aware, free from worries, appears worthy only to be overcome.

Consciously, aspiring children play the popular game of 'becoming grown-up,' which, often unknowingly, becomes a destructive reckoning with the guardian figures of childhood, mistakenly serving as both the template and model for this game.

For the child-seeking, the shipwrecked, it becomes the humiliating game of 'pretending' as they play along with the children. A game that repels, as it often makes a caricature of language, movements, and neglected primitive simplicity. Here, the world of adulthood, driven by willfulness, appears filled with selfishness, corruption, and neglect of the sacred laws of growth and life. If there is indeed blasphemy, then it is the desecration of the holy law of life.

Childhood as a developmental state is something sacred, as it is a segment of the eternally moving life, which no one can halt. In this developmental state, humans are open, natural, without deceit, spontaneous. These qualities, in the process of growing into conscious adulthood, are often overgrown by the accompanying jealousy.

Child-seeking is despicable to the wise, who did not fall victim to jealousy; it is contemptible and abhorrent, as it inherently confesses to the inability to live a mature life.

It may be a source of wonder for the shipwrecked of life that the kings of the world supposedly bowed before a crib. The legend of the giant Christopher, supposedly overwhelmed by a child, is taken as an allegory. Those who hear with delight that a Jewish shepherd boy killed a giant hero with a sling have more understanding of the insult inflicted upon mature humanity when, in the growth of the child, man is beaten.

Childhood!

Whoever had to steel their weapons in the struggle for life may well look back longingly, just as years ago, the joyful message of a new world was sent heavenward. Only those who experienced the inner spiritual battles alongside the life struggle understand this longing fully.

The religions that promise salvation to people, meaning liberation from duty and responsibility in a dreamy afterlife, which already begins — by rejection of the 'earthly,' that is, by dutiful and responsible thinking — in this world, present idle existence as an ideal.

The most zealous followers of these teachings, who have become immature, forgo the creative act reserved for the mature. The creative act includes all dutiful, conscious actions from procreation to warfare. The Tibetan monasteries differ little from those of the monks of Mount Athos or those of the Roman orders. They are all consuming, never productive. They all believe in opposition to the combative, meaning procreative and generative, and thus, in every sense, the fertile world, though they ultimately face unfruitful, childless love in their earnest labors. In their otherworldly realm, filled with the most precious and wondrous ideas, they find an enviable home. For the shipwrecked, they yearn for a harbor that knows no storms and no dangers, a home that means security.

Therefore, it is understandable that in all countries where these otherworldly institutions have established fortified places of idle life, supported by collapsed and shriveled grandeur, the small ones knock at the gates of the walls that separate the world of action from the world of dreams.

That the refuge of the desperate becomes the place of sanctity speaks to all those who remained strong and combative in life, alien, occasionally liberating, though often disheartening.

The mass of the dissatisfied should find a place in these institutions that grants them recognition and enables them to avoid life. Even these 'children' must be reminded of 'growing up.'

Every longing to escape from life — as the demand to fulfill one's duty — is a crime against the law of life itself, even if this longing appears so endearing and is adorned with the most beautiful thoughts and the most radiant images.

Just as in the life of the individual, the law of maturation replaces the state of childhood with adulthood, so too does the same law propel nations from the state of primitiveness to the age of knowledge, of statehood. From the ruins of primitiveness, the age of culture rises, consciously ascending.

Ancient civilizations that long for original, youthful power often fall victim — Rome in its decline is an example — to the error of taking the childishness of foreign nations as an example and end their life's twilight in effeminate decadence. Out of force, they make weakness, out of simple primitiveness, they turn into a void. When childish thoughts take hold in an aging heart, the heart becomes clumsy. Childish words on the lips of adults appear foolish and repulsive.

The longing that looks backward or drives backward is unfruitful. The backward-looking longing of the elderly often mingles with the dread of the hour of death.

'The good old days!'

For many people, the memory of — glorified by distance and therefore blissful — days of youth is the only glimmer of light in the twilight of a shattered life. Their heart has become a museum, which denies entrance to the living spirit and the moving life.

But for those who derive their claim to honor and pride from long-perished and brave ancestors, honor and duty demand to meet the conditions of this honor, to continue the legacy with the same bravery and dedication.

There are also nations that claim the right to respect in the council of nations, without wanting to see that what their forefathers once called culture is now silent, crumbling ruins.

The strong one is well aware of childhood and longing, just as he is familiar with temptation, distress, and doubt.

His memories of childhood are not a mere glow meant to obscure the dark hours of his conscious life but rather represent the thought of that unburdenedness, which calls upon the conscious life for relentless action. For him, the unavoidable question is the direct path of further development, leading solely toward the fulfillment of life's purpose.

Through memory, all those longings that once filled the sails of the ship of life and guided it to the open seas of daring are reawakened and brought to life. Thus, the memory of childhood becomes for the strong an ever-watchful question of conscience regarding the justification of his actions. The plumb line of longing measures both depths and heights, the seas and abysses, the struggles and the descents, over which the knowledgeable and conscious guide steers his ship of life, and measures the heights and skies into which the flight of thoughts and fervent desires ascend.

In memory, childhood becomes, for the strong, that brief moment of carefree dancing and joyful shouting of the still-untamed spirit, which, as an unconditional 'yes' to all manifestations of life, could almost say 'yes' to everything.

And memory brings forth that dangerous, glowing light in the eyes of the strong, before which all who cannot bear to gaze directly into it must look away.

The longing of the strong is acquainted with the weight of the earth and various sufferings of life, yet beyond this weight, it sends arrows of hope into the widely opened heavens of freedom, which, above all abstinence from halves and all gilded cages, voluntarily expands into the imprisonment of a state of surrendering beyond days and nights, extending into the eternity of ideas.

The arrows of hope flew as early messengers into the heavens of longing and announced that the strong one finds himself on a journey to the realm of fulfillment.

Huginn is the name of one of the ravens on Odin's shoulder, the raven of living, world-creating spirit, without which there is nothing that has life. Huginn is the thought bound to action, the knowledge of the strong in the original.

Muninn, however, means memory, the recollection of the pride of strong generations, who were powerful as long as they remained true to themselves and did not open the gates of their kingdom to foreign beings.

And Muninn is the second raven on Odin's shoulder.

Muninn is the forward-looking thought power that gives birth to today's action out of yesterday and tomorrow.

In this 'today,' rooted, encompassing in remembrance and in the orderly unity of original life, our thought grows large, the thought upon which creative action is founded, which gives the strong their world, the world given to their dominion.

Their kingdom has existed for ages and will exist as long as men walk this earth who, driven by longing for perfecting their being, seek unity of soul and reality, harmony of will and worth, as an infallible compass of the infinite in their hearts.

The kingdom of the strong was once a reality. However, under the sign of the cross, in the uprising of the humble and those seeking salvation, the weak and the desperate were pushed out of the realm of the earthly and entered the truly divine realm of the idea, accessible only to the chosen, the strong, the solitary, the skeptics of humility and the faint-hearted security.

The homeland of these few was shifted to this domain. And for the homeland to return to the sphere of reality, the struggle of the solitary and strong of all centuries has persisted since the debasement of strength by humility.

To their hidden homeland, the solitary gave the name 'Freedom.'

And within the word 'freedom,' they encompassed all their longings and dreams, their struggles and actions. Freedom became the inner symbol for the glowing coasts of glory, reawakened by rising power, for the community of the strong and independent, the life-affirming and righteous of the nation.

The secret realm of freedom shone in the eyes of the children, so that even in the solitude of bitter death, they were not abandoned.

The secret realm never had magical formulas, rites, or any ulterior motives; its fraternity was founded purely by the demanding life in freedom.

The secret kingdom of the strong was never bound by a secretive order, though it led the paths of secret knowledge to the source of all power and essence's resilience. Yet, knowledge remained hidden only because the weak, those who thirsted for redemption and yearned for it, had lost sight of the original, having become blind and accustomed to groping for a shepherd's staff for guidance.

The weak no longer had an organ with which they could perceive the light of freedom.

But when the solitary spoke of their luminous realm, the weak were amazed and seemed to hear distant fairy tales. These tales seemed to them as a message from 'once upon a time.' They could not know that these tales were nothing more than tokens of remembrance for the true homeland, the kingdom called freedom.

The Golden Age!

Distorted by the weak, it has here become a land of sloth and there a paradise.

Only those with insight allowed their instinct to tell them that the Golden Age is a reality, which can only be reclaimed through action from the heavens of longing into the realm of existence.

Every solitary soul who hungered for freedom was also a fighter for the new reality of the coming kingdom on this earth. However, this reality does not promise a 'paradisiacal' era, as it is a state of bliss that the weak and other fighters for purposeless adventure seek.

The Golden Age, for which the strong fight, is the reign of justice, which banishes the tyranny of weakness and, in accordance with the law, establishes the order, the worth of originality.

Ovid, whom one could call a Latinic troubadour, speaks of a Golden Age and means thereby that original state which, based on natural law, integrates humans in harmonious essence into the order of the cosmos. The compass of instinct guarantees the 'goodness' of natural humanity, who in unity of simple self-reliant action holds on to the essence of humanity without preconceived notions or hidden agendas.

In his portrayal of the Golden Age, Ovid derives from it the original right and loyal relationship, which meant being 'good' without needing legal proceedings or judgments. In this state, the 'law' becomes merely a 'compass.' The natural understanding does not need to be forced into words; it is practiced independently of dogmas or teachings.

Thus must Nietzsche's words be understood when he calls the great Greek

Plato the 'decadent,' precisely because he brought Greek and, thus, European philosophy to its peak.

Centuries before the light-hearted poet Ovid, the Greek Hesiod portrayed the developmental history of the five ages: the Golden, the Silver, the Bronze, the Heroic, and the Iron Age. In this account lies the lament over humanity's descent from the heights of original essence into the realm of a corrupted, lawless existence, sustained by betrayal, murder, and deceit.

But why did humanity have to fall?

This question arises from the desires, ideas, images, and dream visions of philosophers, poets, statesmen, prophets, and religious founders of all times.

And with the question arises the endeavor to create a new earth and perhaps a new heaven. This recreation aims not only to restore the original, good state but to establish, beyond that, an age purified through suffering and experience.

Yet what should the face of this new humanity look like, which should be the world-image of the renewed creation? Regarding this, opinions, demands, theories, and prophecies diverge widely.

Religious founders had it the easiest, projecting the realm of their promised kingdom onto an unreal, otherworldly plane, where they could govern as they pleased within the realm of fantasy. They did not need to appeal to the ethos, will, courage, or bravery of their followers, but merely to 'faith.' For them, faith was initially submission, an acceptance of their teachings and theories. Then, faith became the organ meant to bind the spiritual and emotional world of the followers to the world of the religious founders.

It's no wonder that through such 'faith,' instinct was deactivated and that, through this deactivation, the compassless heart went astray, believing it had found a new and better home beyond the call of duty, if not the soul itself fell into a trance under the illusion of an imagined haven of grace.

The efforts of Plato and his intellectual school, however, were far more serious. Plato proclaimed in his great vision that the primordial essence inherent in humans is of decisive importance.

For him, it matters whether this essence is gold, silver, bronze, or a lesser metal, and the essence determines human actions, reflecting the responses to appeals from the worthy or unworthy.

Plato's vision knows nothing of grace or merit before 'God' and has no concept of redemption that could reconcile or elevate the essences. Nothing in the world, not even beyond reality, could grant a worthy essence to an unworthy one. Therefore, in this world of appearances, the ultimate wisdom is an unerring selection of those whose essence is worthy. Only the worthy are called to rule. Their core is refined to perfection, while, where impurity prevails, willfulness, chaos, and the destiny of waste come into being.

The world of becoming can, for Plato, therefore, only be a reflection of the eternal ideas, those archetypes that fundamentally structure and determine the essence of humanity. The state is thus the true and visible best, which derives its value from the recognition of original purity and builds itself through the selection of substances.

In Plato's grand images, we feel a breath of the spirit that signifies true eternity: eternity lies where the law prevails, encompassing life and death, rise and decline. The law reveals itself in the strong life, which shows new life and, in its entirety, offers no entry to the seed of decay.

Poets have celebrated this law when they sang of the life of the strong, the heroes, the bringers of light, the victors.

'They sang of youth and love, of bold, golden times, of freedom, manly dignity, of loyalty and sanctity,' as it is called in Uhland's "The Song of the Singer."

The beauty of this golden age lies in the freedom-loving humanity, which, with its proud joyfulness, radiates over dark despotism. Thus, Uhland envisions the Golden Age.

And Walther von der Vogelweide sings of the memory:

'... how we once strove for honor:

Age advised us, the deed belonged to the young!

Now shame overcomes us.

The lesson of the fable that even a child notices:

What follows from it, O wise one, do you find?'

Experience and knowledge, will and action, age and youth belong together in a strong life, and where the living unity of growth is torn apart by despotism, decline follows.

The call for freedom, which poets and singers have raised as harbingers of attack during the darkest hours of the nation, contains at its core, in ever-renewing transformation, the demand for justice, the demand to bring purified values to their rightful place. The struggle against oppression and tyranny is the fight for justice, which is the cleansing of life and the homeland of the strong.

Huginn and Muninn, forward-looking thought power and action-binding memory, together constitute the totality of the spirit. Odin, in the Germanic faith, represents the all-pervading will, through which his spirit's totality pervades creation. Huginn and Muninn are necessary for him to shape his purposeful world plan.

As Huginn and Muninn advise him, so too does the strong one weigh Huginn's and Muninn's utterances in his soul before stepping into action.

When monotheistic Judaism, under the guise of Christianity, 'dethroned' the world to place the LORD of Sinai above it, all sensual elements of Germanic belief, which never desired gods in the sense of a Christian-Jewish theism, were vilified and transformed into caricatures of devils, demons, and heretics.

Where once the strong in the sacred groves, amid the stirring treetops of ancient trees, sensed the rustling of the life-spirit, there where they had their homeland and lived freely in adherence to the law, temples to the honor of a personal god were erected.

The teachings of the law were forgotten, but instead, the message of the 'One God' was exalted, who demanded blind submission and whose favor depended on whether his son and his countless miracles were taken seriously.

The will of the One God, the LORD, sought to displace the wisdom of Odin and even the law itself.

The strong, however, remained loyal to the law and did not bow in worship to the LORD.

They had to endure persecution. One of the deadliest accusations was that they were godless.

The opposite of the theism established on Sinai should be 'atheism.'

'Whoever is not for me, is against me,' proclaimed the LORD, and his servants killed those who were not of the LORD's opinion and who, in defiance, opposed his earthly claim to power.

The Lord from Sinai, Yahweh by name, was always zealous to ensure that no other lord would stand alongside him. His divine peace vanished whenever a Baal somewhere still showed life. And he was extremely sensitive to any 'blasphemy.'

Indeed, a very 'personal' god!

Odin could not be blasphemed, nor could a temple of worship be built for him.

He recognized neither believers nor disbelievers.

Anyone who was strong and knowledgeable in the law, who was upright and lived rightly, endured; whoever was weak and could not fulfill the law perished.

This was neither promise nor threat, neither grace nor wrath: it was life itself!

In the sense of Sinai, all those who, in their philosophy or poetry, in their statecraft or merely in their reality of life, did not adhere to this confession are 'atheists.'

But those who lived by a stronger faith than the so-called 'theists' remained unknown or were silenced.

The strong one has never been a worshiper. Those who see the primary 'service to God' in submission do not forgive him for this. The strong one was strong, or at least great, because of his knowledge of the law in which he stood, strengthened further by the intuition of justice emanating from the law and its order. His actions were the proclamation and orientation toward order, which is why his actions were more akin to 'service to the law' than 'worship.'

Yet the weak never understood the language of the strong, nor their deeds. Thus, the weak feared the strong, and so they conspired to eliminate them and to make their world safe. The sacred trees, symbols of imperishable and eternally renewing life under the law, were consumed by the wrath of the Christians, and Odin's name was cursed as that of a devil.

But the law continued to shine behind the clouds of incense, allowing small, earthy spirits to rise, and the world revived. The weak assumed that grace shone down from a confined heaven rather than the law, yet they could not take a single step out of eternity into the law-imbued universe.

The Lord of Sinai spread the dogma that he created the world from nothing in six days by his word alone. How much greater is the knowledge of the Nordic peoples, who see in Odin the bearer of the all-pervasive law!

Odin gave the law to the churning chaos, thereby imparting meaning and order to the world! — Thus, the elders taught the young to honor the universe and fulfill their duty to humanity.

This is not magic, nor miracle-belief.

Here, the strong one lived by his deed, for creation itself is his deed.

He did not need a god emerging from a burning thornbush to speak Hebrew and give instructions to his chosen people, making them binding upon the entire external world. Nor did he need a LORD in the guise of an angel to go on a journey to the Sodomites, with strange life stories that, in holy tales, are recounted to a believing and wonderstruck humanity.

From Sinai, the world was 'deified' through much violence and legal distortion; however, the truth, this divine law of freedom, was never 'deified' and remained the life-breath of the strong, who stood by the law and lived from it.

The name of Odin was erased from daily language, but the fairy tales murmured his secret from century to century, celebrating his resurrection under various names.

What does a name matter when the idea alone gives life!

Names and designations lead to dogmas, in which the living spirit is pressed to death under the weight of the rigid letters. Perhaps Odin, as the only law that illuminates the heavens of ideas, shines as the all-embracing sun over this universe. And never will little men, fanatical by their religious founders, with heaven-bound ladders of fragile mental systems and ill-constructed religious doctrines, be able to storm the high castle of freedom, which remains the refuge of the strong, where only gods sit on thrones, if there are any.

But whoever speaks of Odin should, in reverence, also report that, as the sagas say, he once sacrificed his eye to drink from the well of Mimir and gain the last wisdom. The final wisdom that Odin could give to the strong, to those whose spirit was of his own, was this:

'All life is struggle, and this struggle is the most fruitful, which can say yes to warriorhood in all its visible forms. Whoever fulfills the struggle of his spirit grows from the tribulations of everyday cares into the pure heights, out of himself forming and establishing creation. The true god among gods lives as part of the whole, ripens with it, and sees in every victory of life his own victory.'

Among the god-stories of all religions, none is as elevating and humbling as this myth of the all-sacrificing Odin, who wanted to impart the will for knowledge, which he shared with the strong.

How different from Yahweh, who in his paradise was keen to be the only one enjoying the fruits of the tree of knowledge, and who cast out those who, in guilt, aspired to knowledge, condemning them and their descendants to grovel without knowledge under the all-knowing Lord.

God-stories arise in the spiritual childhood of peoples. The deepest and wisest stories, however, may be told by the North, not as attempts to turn myths into divine truths or make fairy tales into healing stories.

Even today, the high castle of freedom rises in the North, in the land of midnight, comforting the weary. The sun of the law shines from its towers, inviting the strong to gather under it, to ignore the petty affairs of the mundane world. The homeland of the strong fights for its right to life on this earth and sends out its messengers to proclaim freedom.

Thus, hope returns to a world that had become hopeless.

Hope for a homeland, that is the first ray of sunlight, breaking through the darkness and frightening the servants of gloom.

Hope for a homeland, that is the first phrase of the joyful message that the castle of freedom brings.

Whenever the sun of the law shines indelibly bright?

In the myths of the Northern realm, there is also mention of a Golden Age.

This was, back when Asgard, the garden, the fortress of the Aesir, still existed.

This fortress was the true place of freedom; from it radiated the inexhaustible, warlike power of Odin's all-encompassing spirit, the spirit that is neither bound by time nor space, that fills the world with powerful life, so that it must continuously renew and shape itself.

Since eternity is combative, Asgard could only serve as the homeland of all the strong ones as a fortress and bastion. Here, Odin has his seat. Valhalla is his gleaming hall of heroes, its roof covered with golden shields, with shields hanging from the walls, and every evening the sound of sharpened swords fills it.

Here, the strong, and only the strong, may find a homeland. Here is a god among gods.

This is the heaven of heroes, having nothing in common with the celestial visions of the Jewish patriarch Abraham's bosom, that revered place of the devout.

As long as Asgard towered over the earth, the homeland of the strong remained — intimidating to the cowardly — on this world.

The saga of Asgard's decline is veiled in fateful darkness. The guilt, that is, the absence of the law, crept into the ranks of the Aesir, as the deep mythology of the North tells us.

And through this guilt, the knowledge of the law was lost, allowing ignorance and folly to seep in. Out of blood betrayal comes ruin!

Loki bore, though not from pure Aesir blood, a monstrous and dangerous offspring, the Fenris wolf, and before him Hela, the future goddess of the underworld — half youthful beauty, half decay, an image of life and death in one — and also the Midgard serpent. Thus, in myth, blood betrayal plants the seed of decline. The monsters destroy their creator; their uprising ensures the destruction of the world, which is only sustained through the binding of opposing forces. With Odin disappears the law-giving sense of the cosmos, after which chaos rises in serpent coils.

An inexhaustible wisdom lies in the tragic demise of the pure, law-abiding Baldr, who must die from an innocent throw by a blind man guided by Loki.

Is it any wonder that the new teachings of blood and race arise from the womb of the Northern realm, which produces such myths?

Is it astonishing that the deep wisdom of the pure blood of the strong and worthy is a torment to the weak and unworthy?

Is it so incomprehensible that the law binds forces and, through its order, leads to fruitful effects, confronting the incited opposition of those who would dissolve the 'message' of the law with a promise of 'grace'?

Chaos, which introduces the downfall of the world after the suspension of the law, is accompanied by the crows of the red, the golden, and the black roosters.

The red rooster is the symbol of the Aesir's enemies, the giants. The golden rooster is the symbol of the Aesir, while the black one belongs to the realm of death!

Red, black, and gold!

Thus begins the world fire, after which the new world emerges from the glowing sea.

And a new sun shines over the newly greened earth covered with young green.

On this new earth, however, new people will walk in accordance with the law, after the old people and their old deceit have perished.

The new people will be the strong and the wise who have found their homeland. Their homeland, which is not endangered by betrayal.

This is the comfort and the shining certainty of the strong, who do not tremble in the world fire, who have overcome fear, because they stand in the law, which is life itself.

The knowledge of this deep law imparts more strength than all religions on earth, which try to cloak the 'last days' with their 'revelations.' The teeth have already gnashed, and the idea has already clashed with the sword.

Yet the strong hold the sword and await the resolution. May the nations hold their breath: the North has recognized the law and already sees the new earth behind the clouds of smoke of the world fire! The homeland of the strong will become a new reality. And this reality belongs to the eternity of this world.

'Savants,' whose minds have gone astray, or at best moved in circles, have labored to divide the history of mankind into three phases.

As the first phase, they set the primordial period of the primitive state of nature. Humanity of this time, they opined, existed in childlike, primitive conditions, suitable only for prehistoric investigation. Thus, they wrapped this 'early' humanity pitifully in bearskins and barbarism draped over their shoulders.

The second phase they called the theocentric era, and they brought their loud praise eagerly to this era.

Theocentric: God at the center!

Praise for the theocentric phase of humanity is at the same time a declaration for theocracy, for divine rule.

Divine sovereignty

This means nothing less than the rule of the priestly caste, who, in the name of the wrathful, jealous, and demanding God of Sinai, lay claim to leading and directing the history of this world. The height of the theocratic era is, for them, the Middle Ages, when the total power of the Church dictated everything.

Theocentric is the claim of theology to be the leader of all sciences.

Theocentric is the rule of religion over reason, understanding, instinct, soul, and heart.

Theocentric is the absolute power claim of the Cross over all beings and every expression of life.

One sees that the Golden Age of theocracy is significantly relocated above the songs of the early poets of remembrance!

Theocentric acts the ruler, who, anointed with the oil of grace from the Vatican, seeks counsel from Rome in decisive moments.

All prophets and priests, the scriptural scholars and word interpreters, act theocentrically as they take their directions from the Vicar of Christ and publish them as binding.

The minstrels of the theocracy cannot cease singing the immense merits of the bygone era of the Church's absolute rule, nor cease hoping for a near reestablishment of a new, even grander Golden Age, 'when the time is fulfilled.' For even 'in the last days' they expect a new earth, a kingdom of God, in which Jesus Christ will be the absolute ruler over the living and the dead of all peoples and races.

If we think that on the new earth after the world fire, as the North proclaims, in the midst of a new human race, the reawakened Baldr will dwell among his Aesir brothers to set a solemn memorial to Odin and Asgard, to struggle and downfall, then we will not doubt where the true homeland of the strong will be, if indeed the strong have any choice at all in thought and meaning.

The third phase is designated as the anthropocentric phase. Anthropocentric: humanity at the center!

The historians of the theocracy set the beginning of the anthropocentric phase in the period of the Renaissance, the breakthrough of the Renaissance through the theocentric system.

The unity, that all-encompassing bond of the Church, was torn apart, as they argued, by the life-feeling of the Renaissance, which pushed personality beyond spiritual and bodily constraints of Church power to new rights. They claim boldly that the emancipation from theocracy was equivalent to the separation from God. And outside the Church, under which — politically viewed — God himself resides, there is no salvation!

This revived life-feeling, which turned to earth, its duties and joys, protest and struggle, did not naturally merge with life alone but was also tied to dogmas that became accustomed to and often rebelled against the freedom-curbing law compulsion of the theocrats.

Indeed, the rebellion of the Renaissance must be regarded as a mighty outcry from an oppressed and spiritually stifled soul, newly accustomed to her homeland on this earth.

Nevertheless, a Golden Age has not begun with this rebirth. The fault lies not in breaking away from the cycle around the magnetic pole of 'God,' but rather in the inability to return to the source of all strength, to the law.

Even the rebirth of the spirit, which was to be realized in the field of humanism, ultimately brought nothing but the expansion of education. Only one man from the intellectual sphere of humanism, a German, took the promising step to seek the way to the source: Goethe!

In fact, Goethe found in the brevity of his life the source that became the life symbol of the new homeland of the strong, the secret German nation.

The beauty of the strong life, which still shines even from the pyre and scaffold, whose radiance brings forth core walls and graves, is measured independently of all values of the day, it is measured by the standards of eternal ideas.

The individual, freed from the 'God pole,' could not become 'happier,' as the cries for the return to the earthly Golden Age acknowledge in their dispute. They speak of the bonds of the Middle Ages and do not wish to understand that this 'bond' was complete enslavement, and that a mass of equally shackled people is not a community.

The anthropocentric phase bears all the blame for the dissolution of human community and the dissolution of the last bonds. It is easy to bring evidence to the contrary.

It cannot be assumed that humanism gave rise to rationalism, under which one seeks to pursue an irresponsible pleasure, and which it undoubtedly bore:

A deft juggling with concepts began, which always seemed to bring the undeniable proof that only by returning to Jehovah of Sinai could the necessary and correct connection for this world be found.

The children of divine rule remained in the ruins of their temples and busily set about building new houses of God. Skillfully, they managed to erect 'new buildings' here and there, only to soon realize that these new buildings had been erected on old foundations, and that altars, lamps, and saints' images almost all came from that 'older time,' which the children were ready to quickly reinterpret if needed.

The advocates of rationalism, on the other hand, professed themselves for 'progress' and believed they were approaching a new Golden Age through the constant further development of enlightenment, science, and thought. The confusion of terms was perfect: here thinking of a Golden Age in an attainable future, there a memory of a Golden Age in distant past. Both groups were united only by their fanatical struggle to achieve their goals; one pushed forward violently, while the other retreated with calculated steps.

The reactionaries were the more skillful; they had it easier because their thirst for power was clearly articulated and did not allow many theories, especially no fantasies. For this, they also had the Pope, who regarded the spiritual heritage of the world as connected in a long-since solidified, world-spanning hierarchy. He wanted only one power, nothing but power. The Kingdom of Christ, as he declared, is not of this world.

All the world is subject to Rome," that is its claim, from which it does not concede anything. The entirety of the world is divided into two parts: one part that it possesses and the other that it claims. Its policies are directed toward the return of its, as it asserts, resurrected Lord Jesus Christ. And to ensure that the struggle for this claim is conducted fanatically, ruthlessly, purposefully, and tenaciously, it teaches its followers that the "Last Day," the Day of the LORD, will only come when the entire world bends its knee before the One.

Against this claim, scattered and internally divided groups have arisen, stemming from Rationalism. They seek to bring about the Golden Age and attempt to achieve this with variously shaped "Internationals," whose end goal is a kind of heaven on earth, resembling a more or less moderate communism, whose deadly seed lies precisely in its demand for equality rather than for values.

The "modern" man staggers between the forces of this "Golden Age," which seeks to create a paradise on earth for all eternity, and the "heaven on earth" promised by the Cross, yet nullified by ideas of equality. He does not know whether his greater advantage lies in being "reactionary" in the spirit of the Cross or "revolutionary" in the spirit of equality. He may comfort himself: in any case, he is reactionary!

Let the "learned" heat their heads debating the three phases of human development, and let them decide for this or that Golden Age. Reality has moved forward with the truth of life.

The North has raised its voice and, beyond the trivial disputes of the day, proclaimed its doctrine of race and values. It demands neither retreat nor division, promises neither redemption nor happiness, but calls the world to a spiritual awakening, to a conscious decision.

And if, in later times, "scholars" choose to describe this phase of human history, they may label it "Nation-centric": the nation at the center!

Centered upon and emerging from the nation, this is the thought of the millennium, beginning with the elevation of the spirit to the center of existence.

No "Golden Age" will be ushered in by ringing peace bells, no Hosanna will greet it, and no palms will be laid before it: it draws near upon the battle trail, followed by armed men who are ready, with sword in hand, to seek homeland and the right to live.

The striving forces have bound themselves anew to the unity of a community of destiny, fulfilled by the same blood, the same longing, the same will, seeking the path to freedom.

Nation-centric! The sons of this world fulfill their homeland with a new vitality, for they do not wish to establish a dormant paradise on earth but strive instead to establish a just order, according to which the strong are called to leadership. Not for the glorification of their own fame, not for the exaltation of a god's glory, not for the fame of a people, but solely for the eternal life of the nation, into which the lives and honor of all merge.

Instead of a "messianic figure," there arises the deification of humanity, which finds its highest expression only in the binding of individuals to the nation.

A blazing and clear image of the blossom of each nation emerges, to be this earth's mighty, growing image of life.

The beauty that radiates from this image will be the masculine and warlike beauty of those who, like the heroes of Asgard, stand firm.

It is deeply rooted, this longing for homeland, and in a fruitful spring all the arrows of hope point towards this coming Reich.

The homeland of the strong, the realm of freedom, is not a utopia, for the boundary posts are within reach for everyone whose will combines with knowledge and memory, whose blood remains pure to perceive the language of the soul and the whispers of the heart.

Only in Germany, as the land of the North, could that wonderful song of mysticism resound, which—despite much obscuration—has contributed to breaking the bond of servitude between Lord and servant that was proclaimed at Sinai as the relationship between God and man.

The Germanic man knows no bowing, no casting oneself into the dust, no kowtow. Neither before the Lord of this world nor that world.

It is unworthy and offensive to him to serve a god like a worm or to demonstrate servile sentiments, which, however, is called "humility."

Thus, as a free and equal, he also dismisses all mediators and intercessors as intermediaries.

Master Eckhart sang his chant, and the memory he reminded us of was the unity between "God" and man. For one thing is certain: the wills of all beings who come from the One are united.

In a religious sense, therefore, the strong are God's brothers, never his servants or immature children or even his sheep!

The brotherhood of all the strong reaches up to heaven and holds fast. Fallen heroes, the initiates, sit in the seats as equals, as comrades, as brothers at a common table and drink from the same cup with them.

From the gods, the heroes derive their lineage. Through the clouds of the solstice night that envelops them like a wreath, Eckhart saw Valhalla, where he saw the brotherhood of "God's children," from which the fifth line binding to the All originates.

And in Valhalla, all the religious rebels who no longer wanted to bow their knees and no longer wanted to lower their necks saw in their spirit, for they desired to see the face and eye of the god who wished to command them.

The homeland of the strong is filled with the brotherhood, alive under the commandments of the honor of warriorhood.

There is no equalizing collective, no clashing cult of individual heroes, but rather the great bearing and powerful community of those whose life manifests itself not in a single act, but in continuous creation.

Therefore, the millennium of the strong is not a paradise, for paradise can at best be a maintained state, but it is a powerful life, surrounded by earthquakes, fires, places of storms and tempests, where the weak perish, but where the strong become even stronger!

In this longing, in the longing for danger and trial, the thirst for life emerges from boyhood, from the untouched. But once the homeland of the strong has been found, immortality of the idea grows within them.

Mysticism, like Romanticism, knew dreams and sighs and often could come to terms with "good thoughts" rather than action. But there is no place in the homeland of the strong for this, for the stance manifest in this world is the stance of heroic realism. Therefore, at the head of the strong stands Odin, on whose shoulders sit Huginn and Muninn, and Odin's thoughts are neither world-weary nor occasionally embellished with fantastical or dark hues. He who stands there is conscious of responsibility and foresight, simultaneously tender and yet filled with bold care, only watching over the strong, leaving behind the weak.

Thus, the stance of heroic realism can be broadly outlined.

It is the arm that draws the bow from which the arrows of hope fly into the land of longing.

And can the weakling ever draw the bow? He must remain in the baseness of his instincts and ask a merciful god for the grace to let the dim light of grace shine upon the haze of his lowliness.

In especially humiliating moments, however, the weak ask that the sun of grace may also shine upon their enemies, the strong! But those who look into the clear radiance of the one sun of the law laugh at all pity.

They have no fear of coming too close to the sun, for they themselves are fire from fire and light from light.

They hear the harmony of the spheres and are filled by the tones of the great unity of the law, therefore they do not succumb to the seductions of the senses, whose songs appear to them only pitiable and discordant. Whoever, in the orbit of the eternal law, pulls his path through the stars like them, does not stray from the path, for he is fortified against temptation and betrayal.

Thus, injustice recedes from the homeland of the strong.

It is pointless to ask whether the strong will ever deify this earth. It is enough to recognize that the strong will wrest the conditions for the rebirth of life through the law.

The time is not far when the strong will receive their homeland. That will come when the earth offers space for its just dominion.

Then their youth and longing will shine out into the new day.

CHAPTER

2

THE DESIRE FOR ROLE MODELS

The time of childhood, with its protective shelter, lies behind us. The maturation into humanity never occurs without pain and suffering, disappointment, and renunciation. Indeed, maturation is often interwoven with pangs, much like a birth. And perhaps it is good and beneficial that a person falls from heaven to heaven until they land on this earth with both feet. Surely, it is also conducive to maturation when a person, on their journey, is expelled from every paradise they have constructed out of reservations and considerations, out of carelessness and cunning. This is the true and sole grace that life has to grant: that it lets people wander and keep wandering until one day they find a home, and this home is their heart, which teaches them the law.

If memory has a profound meaning, it is this: to keep alive human longing—

the demand for wandering. The great wandering is the fate befitting the Nordic race. Not that destructive, restless, and hunted wandering of nomadic, parasitic races, but that powerful wandering of the soul that continually strives for new goals and insights, that creative restlessness that might appear demonic and terrifying to the non-Nordic world. This creative restlessness is just as palpable among the Vikings and the culture-creating Nordic tribes, who spread across the world to be the seeds of abundantly sprouting peoples—as we read in the myths of non-Aryan peoples, who speak of the white sons of gods from the North—as it is palpable in the ecclesiastically constrained centuries of the Middle Ages. And there, where freedom found its last refuge in scholars' studies, world-shaking ideas emerged from humble attic rooms.

This is the sacred restlessness of the Germans, who have preserved the legacy of the Viking spirit in its purest form among all Nordic peoples. It comes alive in the Hanseatic League, in the bold ideas of Jürgen Wullenwever, the rebellious Lübeck citizen; it pushes forward in the heart of the Great Elector, just as it does in the statesmanlike ideas of Frederick the Great. In Nietzsche, it shatters the conceptual constructs of a weary world. It transforms citizens into soldiers, escaped monks into rebels, and scholars detached from the world into heaven-storming explorers.

Every historical account remains fragmentary if it does not start from this German demon, the sacred restlessness—and from its antagonists. Fortunate is the state that knows how to harness this creative restlessness into its sails, steering towards immortality, for it embodies totality within itself.

German restlessness does not give birth to the desire for novelty that is characteristic of many peoples, particularly the Romanic race. Nor is dissatisfaction a trait of the restless and longing German blood. Rather, the sacred restlessness is the ever-awake growth and maturation, the mysterious premonition of the dangers of complacency and bliss. Therefore, the North has never been a place of bloodthirsty revolutions; instead, it has always been under the sign of inexplicable fermentations and tensions.

The German nation needs only one revolution, but a total one—the revolution towards itself.

For centuries, crusts and foreign layers have accumulated on the German essence, seeking to obscure the law. In the total revolution, all these layers should be shed to "turn the lowest to the highest" in the best sense. This is also contained in the literal meaning of "revolution." The total German revolution is committed to the noble purpose of creating a new people.

Since the creation of a people is an eternal process of growth, the bearers of the German revolution are full of restlessness and demand. Thus, the total revolution of the Germans is never nihilistic but is always and constantly subjected to a higher purpose—namely, to grow into the perfection of the law. Judged from this perspective, heroic realism is the compass needle that guarantees, in every case, that the lawful direction is maintained.

By nature, the number of the strong who understand the law is small. Ultimately, it is only the few—the chosen, the incorruptible—who become leaders of the masses and imprint their understanding of the law upon their people's environment.

However, through a healthy instinct that recognizes these few leaders and carries the desire to join them on the path to the future, a people decide on life, ascent, and greatness. It is telling that true leaders never promise the people heaven on earth, but rather a life in true freedom and the duty of humanity.

In the adherence to the shown goals, a people divide into the longing and the greedy. The times of disgrace, humiliation, impotence, and shame have always been when, instead of a leader, a demagogue could arouse the instincts of the greedy. The fact that these times often required voluntary deprivation, even conscious poverty, turned greed into a crime and the demagogue into a vile criminal, sometimes even a murderer.

The desire for role models has always been alive in the Nordic realm, and it is a sign of the spiritual greatness of the North that the standards it applied to role models were tremendous. In heroic songs, long before the Nibelungenlied, all the wishes and ideas that the longing had of their role models, who were supposed to lead to action, were embedded. And anyone who believed they could fulfill these prerequisites, to be a role model themselves, could measure from these demands how close or far they were from the praised deed.

To this day, the fundamental theme of Nordic-inspired poetry is the exceptional, the unique—that is, the heroic life. This poetry has always reignited the fire of enthusiasm in the young and old longing, illuminating their way home during dark hours.

In times of decline, Jewish or Jewish-influenced writers began depicting states of non-heroic life. Their descriptions were often skillfully written and frequently engaging to read. However, instead of longing, they contained greed; instead of courage, impudence. They praised not the brave overcoming of obstacles as life's wisdom but sly evasion of them. By "Jewish," we understand the cunning tactics toward life aimed at gaining advantages in all circumstances, even in disgraceful conditions. This does not aim at enhancing life's sense by acquiring new and elevated spiritual value, but at rummaging through the slag heaps of inherited conditions for usable remnants.

However, where this Jewish spirit created clever life theories, as in Marxism, it developed systems for the advantageous international division of all available material and ideal goods.

The Nordic spirit, in contrast, pursued the goal of creating, through the teaching of lawfulness, a decisive tool for refining the metals within man, allowing the strong to become aware of their strength, thus enabling creativity and fertility. In doing so, it established the prerequisites for rightful rule.

Thus, Nietzsche was the first conscious counterweight to the calculating and speculative Jewish spirit that exploits situations, satisfying the desire for role models with the demand for the Übermensch, the total person, the lawful person. Here, minds could diverge—and they did so thoroughly.

Let it never be forgotten that one of the best and most valuable inheritances in the Nordic racial soul is the Viking spirit. Born from creative restlessness, the Viking spirit gave the sedentary farming people a yearning for breadth and action in their blood, thus preserving them from the danger of spiritual stagnation—a danger that befell many farming peoples lacking the inheritance of restlessness.

The Viking spirit particularly reveals the creative demon of Nordic people. The hard, brave, and knowledgeable men who sailed the seas in their small, seaworthy ships, versed in astronomy and familiar with mathematical calculations, did not only bring back treasures as the spoils of their perilous journeys, unlike the marauding hordes of Asia, but they also founded settlements and states. For mighty rulers, it was a particular honor to have honor guards from this chosen race.

The young warriors of the North chose leaders whom they intended to follow into the limitless expanses of manly, creative action. More than the prospect of honor, fame, and gain, they were driven by the desire to have duties, to bear responsibility, to provide valid evidence of outstanding competence.

The law of the North can be mirrored no more beautifully and clearly than in this moral code of longing and restless young warriors.

The desire for role models stemmed from the wish to mobilize all existing values through the leader. The leader was not only permitted but was required to demand the highest and ultimate. The goal was to emulate him in life and death. The awareness of being a role model in all things compelled the leader to surpass himself, to become a hero.

Later, when the path into the wide world was walled off by foreign powers, the longing were often left with brave death as proof of a warrior's spirit, as courageous life was made nearly impossible by the systematically induced confinement.

It is noteworthy that, for example, a large part of the pre-war officers were always ready to set a brave example for soldiers led to the battlefield, but little courage was seen in their lives during the preparation times for war. This ultimately led to the widespread dangerous notion that a soldier, and especially an officer, was only worth something in wartime. The heroic death was stamped as the "profession" of the warrior, while the heroic life became undesirable and even detested in the satiated and tired times.

One of the most significant accomplishments of the outstanding military thinker Ludendorff, who highlighted the significance of the military life so profoundly in his book on total war, was to thoroughly dismantle this mad notion. His phrase, "Strengthen the soul of the people," will one day stand as a beacon over the military awakening of the National Socialist era.

The strong state, which strives for totality, knows the unavoidable necessity of providing young, longing people with the opportunity to satisfy the desire for role models. It understands that the Nordic race remained so capable of life only because—even with the artificial suppression of the heroic ideal by the type of the sufferer—a hidden selection process took place, continually choosing the stronger type. In superior action, the strong have even in their hour of death been able to issue an appeal to the longing, planting the seed of readiness for action. And this seed particularly took root where the most inhospitable living conditions prevailed, where people gladly turned away all prospects of profit to avoid walling off their homeland.

The realization of the desire for role models is only possible when there is no gap between the idea and the appearance of the role model on one hand, and on the other hand, when the role model, through the living example of their action, is able to influence the will of the longing. The current of the personality of the role model is only closed when the longing devote themselves from recognition, through dedication to grow greater, placing themselves in the hands of the role model as the living tool of his firmer will and clearer vision without depersonalizing themselves.

From this alone arises loyalty.

But loyalty is always a reciprocal relationship. There is no one-sided loyalty. At best, that would be obedience. But obedience is also found in despotisms.

Greater than all obedience and more reliable than even the best-trained discipline is the knowing loyalty of those who have entrusted themselves to the role model for better or worse.

This contains the secret of the victories of numerically smaller groups, sworn in loyalty to the role model, over armies.

Calculating wisdom can indeed bring about commitment and action. But the success of wisdom is called into question if the outcome appears uncertain.

Loyalty might seem "old-fashioned" to the merely clever. But the total state, which grows into eternity from this world through harmony with the law, can achieve a hundredfold through loyalty what the liberal state can achieve through cleverness.

The more a people can create role models for their longing, the greater will be the number of loyal followers who emulate the leader guiding them to the heart of the nation.

One should consider that theories may inspire dreamers to die, but ideals are only achieved when leaders teach by their living example that realization is possible and worth experiencing.

The leader becomes the organ through which the idea is taken out of the realm of unreality and brought to life. And the more vividly people can represent an image of the eternity of the nation through their actions, the more alive a people's present becomes.

Despotism is content to rule over blindly obedient people and, if necessary, uses the effective tool of fear. Its agents are the enforcers and bailiffs who wield command power. The uniformity of "conviction," which is essentially just quick assent to often incomprehensible commands, is supposed to guarantee the preservation of the demanded state. Thus, despotism can only confront the desire for role models with the disciplinary rod of the drillmaster, leading the longing through enforced submission.

Despotism exhausts itself in the enjoyment of power in the moment and views the future with concern. Every growth is dangerous to it. It is no coincidence that the roots of despotism, even the spiritual kind, have their nurturing ground in the Orient. The North could never have brought forth today's world religions, and it was a condemnation of the longing souls when the doctrines born of the spirit of Sinai claimed command over the souls of Nordic people.

The total state, the living expression of the people's will to wholeness, grows into power by fostering the diversity of the strong instead of uniformity, paving the way to rule for the strongest through selection. It gives the longing souls the opportunity to act and thus proclaims to them the right to homeland. Because the path to the goal is shown through knowledge of the law, the total folk state is free from the dangers of chaos, deviation, and confusion.

The law gives no answers to the oracle-seeker who seeks counsel for specific cases but imparts knowledge to the longing soul: nothing in the world of ideas and appearances is based on grace or miracles. Everything that moves the world, everything that carries life and gives life, is an expression of the law, which never breaks itself. In the human soul resides the organ that connects him to the law. Instinct and will, blood and knowledge, in their harmony, create the tone that merges into the great harmony of the law. Where inner discord makes the tone impure, the organ closes itself off and no longer perceives the harmony of the law. The final struggle of man is for inner purity, for the preservation of harmony, for the annihilation of all counterforces of mixing that lead to disharmony. The degree of inner purity determines the degree of perfection in growing into and becoming at home in the law.

To Judaism and its offspring, Christianity, the "desire to be like God" was the premise for original sin because the "godlikeness" of man necessarily abolishes the lord-servant relationship between God and man. On this relationship, however, Judaism and Christianity build their religions, and even the softer description of Christianity as a "father-child relationship" does not change this basic orientation, which inevitably leads to the dependency of humanity. This means weakening. The comfort of these religions merely fills people with a begged-for "semblance of strength."

In contrast, the person who stands in the law is as strong as life itself, beyond fear, and submits neither to "providence" nor to fate, nor even to the counsel of a personal god. Since his inner harmony connects him with the harmony of the law, he is part of the great law itself, and thus he is "like God."

Even in times when the knowledge of the law was lost, the foreboding, the memory, remained. Even the diverted thinking of the greatest theologians from the North, who circled around "the god" who could fill people to the point of brotherhood with him, ended in heresy against Sinai and the Bible of the Old and New Testaments. Heresies were and remained all those currents that merged in "mysticism" and "pantheism." Again and again, the law manifested itself in the strong, who became heralds of freedom. Thus, the memory remained alive. For centuries, the North was ravaged by battles, but whenever it called for the fight for freedom, it was moved by the rhythm of the law.

The history of the North resembles a fever curve, which, after life-threatening crises, after high temperatures and frighteningly low temperatures, returns to the health point of the law.

Indeed, the oracle at Delphi was opposed to Nordic thought, but the saying that shone upon the pilgrim from the sanctuary was a word of the law:

Know thyself!

The call to reflection is the first step toward a mindset, toward knowledge of one's own law. From here arises understanding, that gateway which leads to the homeland of the strong.

The strong become role models because they are the image of the law! The law is that force which governs life and death, arising, passing away, and becoming anew, whose origin lies beyond human perception. Aligning oneself with its harmony is the ultimate longing of those who understand. Only the strong are capable of uniting the resonance of their soul with the great harmony of the universe, because neither the hope for reward nor the fear of the overwhelming power of fate can cloud their pure sense of the greatness of the law.

The instinct of the strong points them, like a magnetic needle, toward the pole of strength. Thus, the strong also know the "right moment" for their action. They are believers in knowledge! They can find the right path through their will, a path that even a miracle cannot reveal to the weak.

The law is greater than all "dear gods" that fearful people have created as a comfort for their weakness. The law is itself greater than all conceptions, for it is the seed of all life, the primal will of all phenomena. Distance from the law is therefore worse than any "godlessness"!

The law can no more be captured in dogmas than the sun in sacks. Toward it, there is neither "belief" nor "unbelief," only the will toward the perfection of action or instinctless persistence in actionless, fearful contemplation.

To stand within the law means to lead oneself to perfection; what are all fear-filled prayers in comparison? Will, research, and instinct, the language of the blood, teach the lawfulness of life, which is part of the lawfulness of the universe. And human wisdom tells him to live lawfully, to preserve life itself.

Understanding the law teaches the strong to hate everything that is hostile to the unfolding of life. Whoever lives within the law is strong; and where a person consciously acts within the law, they grow beyond themselves.

The expression of life in the strong, their bearing, arises from this knowledge of the law, which compels people to effectiveness and leads to an exalted security of life feeling, to dignified calm and superior pride.

In the age of confusion, of distance from the law, the resolute defiance of solitude has often carved hard lines around the mouths of the strong. But the more the homeland of the strong once again takes possession of this earth, the more the solitary gain that serene cheerfulness, which is the true mirror of a law-conscious soul.

In contrast stands the nervous haste of those who wander aimlessly, consumed by misguided instincts. The feeling of insecurity frightens their will and subjects it to moods from which no action can ever be born.

The insecure, the weak, attempt to replace the missing rhythm with teachings and dogmas, religions, "salvation foods," "elixirs of immortality," and similar means to create a sense of life security through this substitution. When they succeed, they are often led to arrogantly claim the infallibility of their methods and teachings, which they gladly present as universally salvific.

However, the longing never allows itself to be given a substitute for life by doctrine, nor can dogmas ever satisfy their desire for role models.

Wherever the homeland of the strong becomes reality, redemption religions recede before ethics. Where the truth of the law demands that the strong be made stronger, redemption religions die.

There, the North triumphs over the Orient. There, the light of the midnight sun overpowers the smoke of Sinai.

The desire for role models continually drives the longing to disregard the phantoms and idylls of "happiness" that lie beyond the path to the goal.

Happiness, after all, tempts one to passive contentment, to "coziness," and thus growth, maturation, and, in short, life, cease.

The strong of all ages have never seen "happiness" as the continuation of a beloved state but as duty, struggle, and great transformation. Neither possession nor power were in themselves desirable, but only effectiveness. They fought their struggle for freedom to fulfill the law in creative ways.

Thus, the strong in their expressions of life are "unromantic."

The heroic realism of the strong life works not with moods but with demands.

For the sake of demands, the longing adheres to role models. They are the beacons illuminating the way through darkness until the dawn of the early morning.

The songs of the longing are neither polished nor smooth like those of dreamers who lie in the grass and gaze at the sky. They are brittle, rough, and full of a magnificent austerity, like the path the longing follows.

The songs that praise the "happiness" of the strong are songs of battles and struggles.

The strong know that an idea without a sword is a dream, just as a sword without an idea is a lifeless piece of iron.

The joy of life, the knowledge of the magical powers of the will, enlivens the dead and gives the thing a soul. Without joy of life, however, the living is dead.

Where the longing steps forward in search of role models, the world is experienced. A new spring, an awakening of creative instincts, passes over this earth.

The wish "to become better" lifts the hearts of the longing. To become better means for them to grow further into the perfection of the law until its fulfillment. For them, moral goodness is the purity of the law. Their morality, therefore, is not compassion, for all compassion implies a lowering, a descent into the sick. Rather, their demand is a call for the strong to brotherhood in the journey and the goal.

Whoever leads the longing to freedom knows the secret of success: it is to awaken and keep alive the noble passions, the passions that can topple gods and tear down heavens if heavens and gods conspire against freedom.

The noble passions, once awakened, are themselves what inflame the will for ever higher flights into new worlds.

The will, in union with the soul, begets the bold thought that knows no obstacles, no discouragement, that finds its home in the universe and places the image of the universe into the smallest being and the smallest thing.

The boldness of thought once gave humans wings, allowing them to rise from earthly dust into the pure light of the clouds.

It was left to Nordic humanity to dream the dream of Daedalus and Icarus and to conceive the myth of Wayland the Smith, just as it was left to them to realize this boldest of human dreams in creative action.

Where the strong became so great and solitary that role models lagged behind, they became seers. They were given to behold the great light of the law. Their vision was holier than all prophecies of the world.

But the North could never invent redemption religions because it sought fulfillment in the reality of the world and did not yearn to leave reality for heavenly ladders.

The role model could only be the leader into the reality of the law, never the prophet calling them into the realm of dreams.

The law of eternal becoming itself has driven the strong to carry out a selection process through role models and the longing, ensuring that even in times of death, at least one bearer of life could step into a near future.

Many races had to die because, after their twilight of gods, they could not gaze upon a new earth with even a single survivor; their blood could not celebrate resurrection because their will to live had perished. The Aryan race has been able to rise again despite countless changes because the solitary kept the secret of the law hidden in caves and on mountains, guarding it as a sacred legacy until the daybreak when the longing set out to discover the secret of freedom and proclaim it to the world.

Christianity, in its will to destroy the law, showed radical cleverness. It cast the natural human into hell to resurrect a "second Adam." In every baptism, it enacts the symbolic death and symbolic resurrection. But the second Adam is the truly "selfless" human, the human without individual will, without inner self, without identity, without spirit. The original spirit is banished so that the spirit of the Lord may fill it.

The "fulfillment" that Christianity preaches is passive. The fulfillment, however, that the strong experience by growing into the perfection of the law, is the most active imaginable.

To entirely abandon oneself to be filled with the spirit of the Lord is the mysterious interpretation of the miracle of the outpouring of the Holy Spirit. And whoever, by Christian belief, is filled with this Holy Spirit speaks a third language, is a third race. Blood, will, race, language no longer matter; only the being filled with the foreign, impersonal spirit, the Holy Spirit of the Lord, counts. The second Adam now walks the earth as a guest until his final "salvation," and everything that reminds him of the time of the first Adam is "sin."

Indeed, Christianity's method of annihilating personality is astonishingly bold, even daring to seek out and slay the first Adam in the hidden recesses of one's most secret thoughts. Repentance, penance, confession of sins, and vicarious forgiveness are effective means of tracking down and destroying the old self. Giving oneself wholly to the Lord and His Spirit is the highest joy of the Christian who has lost their self. Submission to the will of the ONE, equating to submission to those who represent Him, is the highest morality! And the targeted policy of the cross is obedience to the command to conquer the world for the Lord.

This principle has been chosen by clever people for realization; otherwise, the successes of this law-opposing movement would not be so surprising.

How much greater, then, will be the victory of the strong for the homeland when one considers that the strong defend the law, thus being rooted in the natural, and do not require unnatural self-renunciation but rather must fight for the fulfillment of their self.

The politicians of the cross know that their mortal enemies have arisen in the law-bound, freedom-loving strong, who set about establishing order on this earth. They fear that the desire for role models will one day lead the longing to rise in revolt, to fight for the homeland of the strong. Hence, their praise is directed to the weak and the humble, who are promised heaven. Hence, their curse is directed at all that is strong, which, like Lucifer the light-bringer, is to be cast out.

The desire for role models drives the longing into an ever-renewed struggle for perfection. The wish to become stronger even tempers impulses so that even in pleasure the sanctity of will casts its light. The longing wishes for sons as heirs to the fight for freedom and feels eternally connected to the creative law through children and grandchildren.

Christian asceticism, which knows nothing of the inherited struggle and bears the curse of original sin, can see only sin in pleasure, as it lacks any understanding of the higher purpose of procreation. This also dictates its view of women: the strong see in her the holy guardian of motherhood, while the Christian sees only the source of sin and temptation.

The time has come when the message of the strong no longer falls on deaf ears. And the time has come when maternal women rise to advocate for the honor of pregnancy and to rebuke the offensive word about defilement.

May it be recognized and never forgotten what it means for the men and women of the North when the Christian Savior is said to have been born of an "immaculate" virgin, who remained a virgin even after birth until her death!

The law crowns the strong with the crown of perfection. This means that the law does not create a new, a second human. The person of pure blood, who is capable of wielding the sword of the spirit and hurling the spear of will, does not need to be redeemed from their body; rather, they require the constant strengthening of their gifts into perfection until, in the flight of their soul, they can behold the light of the law. Only the character of a personality that has retained its self can stir and steer its wings.

Here the gulf opens between the strong and the humble. The humble believe that humanity's ultimate purpose is to glorify and praise God, relegating humanity to the cozy sphere of pious contemplation. The strong, however, know that humanity can only be realized in the effectiveness of the law, in the knowledgeable order in which the strong must place the world of accessible phenomena.

The strong have not received a mission from a LORD to lay the "world" at His feet. Rather, the strong know themselves to be called to be bearers of the law and upholders of order. Thus, their humanity rests in the constant struggle for knowledge of the law and its effects.

The wisdom of the strong is readiness to grow, is being awake to the voice of longing, is being able to see the effect of the law. The action of the strong is the sword that gives reality to wisdom. Reality, however, means life for the strong and death for the weak.

The reality of the strong has given its commands and orders, creating—beyond the laws of Sinai—a chivalrous morality that can respond to all needs and demands of existence: bring yourself into harmony with the law and fight so that your nation becomes the homeland of the strong!

Chivalrous morality cannot be learned like a creed or a prayer. Nor does it create priests. It can only send teachers into the world to show people the way to their own hearts. It can only choose strong individuals as leaders who can satisfy the longing for role models.

Thus, priestly rule will perish when the strong take over the spiritual guidance of the longing. The spiritual guidance of the longing will then consist in the proclamation and acceptance of the wisdom of the strong. Thus, justice, as the expression of the inner order of the law, returns to the homeland of the strong.

Justice consists in placing values in the "correct order." Where the external order of things and beings does not correspond to the law, arbitrariness with its devastating manifestations and consequences inevitably arises.

Times distant from the law have attempted to "elevate" people through "education." It was thought that one could make a person "free" by indiscriminately filling them with all kinds of cheap "knowledge." The result was only that such a person became demanding to the point of insolence, fundamentally discontented, a pursuer of advantages, and thus ultimately unfree.

The "elevation" of humanity rather consists in each person coming to effectiveness within the community of the people according to their nature. Thus, justice becomes the ruler. There is a supreme wisdom of the state, which can become the expression of the homeland of the strong: to recognize the values of people, to see them, and thus to make use of them. Values without effectiveness are theory. Therefore, where the strong strive for the wholeness of life and secure a homeland, the total state arises as the best means to a higher purpose from the perspective of the highest utilization of values.

Because true culture can only arise where the unity of life has been achieved through knowledge of the law, the total state is the first cultural state.

Its task is to protect the spiritual guidance of the longing from every encroachment of the weak, who are only capable of creating confusion. It is the living shell around the seed of the nation's eternal life. The desire for role models finds its effective fulfillment in the longing following their leaders in service to the state. Their perfection will be demonstrated in the perfection of the state, which unfolds into totality through their service.

The longing to bring oneself to effectiveness in duty and thus fulfill one's own law places the strong far above the ambitious, whose motivations are vanity and greed.

The ambitious know no desire for role models and thus have no desire to be role models themselves. No community is possible with them, as their will is without character. They can never be heralds of freedom and fighters for an ideal, as they would only use the ideal as a cloak for their personal pursuit of power. Power that is not oriented toward community and nation results in arbitrariness and despotism.

Ambition that manifests in the lust for power leads to disloyalty in those possessed by it, as they seek out the company of men only to use them as tools to achieve their goals. Once they reach their goal, they betray their tools.

Ambitious revolutionaries have led nations to ruin, whereas role models, who led men to freedom, were able to raise nations to the heights of true power.

It is the wisdom of the total state to separate the longing from the ambitious and to entrust the administration of the people's heritage to the strong.

Where the strong have found the way to their heart, they grow into personalities. And where personality realizes its law, it becomes fruitful in the community.

The nation to which the longing of the strong belongs is full of life.

The state that provides a homeland to the strong is full of life. The will to act, which sows eternity, is full of life.

CHAPTER

3

OF MEN & THEIR WORK

The restless North was the last stronghold of freedom because it was also the solitary nest of strong men who frightened the lawless world through their interpretations and their fierce, unheard-of will to live. And particularly the restless, interpreting German appeared to the old, dying world as a demon who constantly assailed the walls of the false order, who instinctively set fire to the decaying temples as a heretic, who mocked dogmas—the "revelations" of unspirit—and who, as a rebel from the joy of life, opposed the "system," the arbitrary "order" born of weakness and false wisdom, and, knowing the law, defiantly and provocatively danced out of line. The new science of the lawfulness of spirit and ideas will provide evidence that the solitary rebels of the previous millennium, the demonic rebels, were the true heralds of their time. It will topple idols and overturn many sanctimonious altars, but, above all, it will be able to delineate the spiritual and emotional territories of the homeland of the strong.

From this perspective, it is worthwhile to examine Plato's striking demand for the inclusion of philosophers in government.

The spirit of an age is determined by the atmospheric vibrations of the law, which the strong capture.

The greatness of a man lies in making his deeds the voice of the law. His tempered will is the metal that clearly and purely transmits the tone of harmony.

Genius, however, is the valid and perfect revelation of the law in its time.

The knowledge of the lawfulness of its creative life has driven genius to struggle against hostile forces throughout history. The awareness of its "mission"—that is, obedience, the fulfilling bond to the law—has compelled genius, without regard for persecution and scorn, to complete its work stone by stone, reflecting a precise plan mirrored in the contemporary thought that directs reason towards creation.

From its solitary height, genius has proclaimed its vision of the great connections. Where small minds saw only seemingly insurmountable walls, under it spread the heights and depths, the hidden places, abysses, and chasms of the world of phenomena like a map. Where small minds saw broad cracks and chasms, dividing rivers and seas, genius saw the unifying and ordering entirety and wholeness of the law.

When small minds knelt in worship before fragments of understanding, genius, in its knowledge of the inexhaustible, all-encompassing greatness of the law, could mock those who set out to capture light with mousetraps and believed they had safely stored the radiance of truth in sacks forever.

To small minds, genius must always appear destructive, just as a child is both outraged and saddened when proud buildings rise where it played in the sand yesterday.

The child will never want to understand that its playground, its paradise, must give way to serious work. Weeping and complaining, it watches as one day the stone it knew so intimately, which perhaps meant the entire world to it, becomes a tiny part of a massive foundation.

To childish people, it may seem cruel that the construction of the work, the realization of ideas and plans that the law commands through genius, takes no account of children's tears, children's dreams, or children's plans. A broken doll does not signify the end of the world, only the end of a foolish illusion. Just as a builder would be mad if he built his walls zigzagging around the playgrounds of sad children, so too would genius have missed its moment if it obscured the reality of its vision for the sake of romantic dreams.

The attitude of genius has always been conditioned by heroic realism. This realism includes an unconditional courage for truthfulness. But without heroism—that believing and knowledgeable "nevertheless" that overcomes resistance—realism would lack its offensive weapon.

Truly great ideas and works have grown from heroic realism. "Faith" alone has never moved mountains; it has only suggested their removal.

———————————————

The Homeland of the Strong is the Birthplace of Genius.

While in the previous millennium, genius was often excluded from shaping earthly matters and had to limit itself to writing its plans for posterity in the stars, the homeland of the strong brings the realization of the idea.

The weak and the half-hearted have perished against obstacles and failures; the strong have knowingly advanced into the ultimate solitude. But now, they will gather from dispersion and return to their homeland as victors.

The ignorant will freeze in astonishment when they realize that death could not conquer genius, that instead, it raises its spirit as a living witness from the grave on the day when the separated parts of the universe—heaven and earth—unite into a new wholeness through enlightenment, error, and crime.

The twilight of the gods is over; the North brings with its understanding of the law the new earth, where the strong will have a homeland.

The old and dying world still does not understand the tremendous event taking place in the heart of the North. Even many witnesses to the new reality do not yet see the law that is shaking the North. In despair, they sense doom where the pains herald the birth of the knowledgeable human.

It is the pride of knowing Germany to be the birthplace of the eternal nation, which rises above all half-measures, errors, and imperfections of the moment. The human soul has broken free from the grip of the dungeon, shattered all chains binding heart and mind, and once again fills the strong, making them the executors of the law.

What are all curses, condemnations, and slanders compared to this fact!

The present moment, with its temptations, is the hour of trial, where the half-hearted and corrupt fail and perish. But the strong, in their moment of victory, look over the earth and its history, seeking examples and warnings.

To this very day, a figure haunts the earth, claiming to be a guide toward perfection. Millions of people bow in reverence before the figure of the Jewish revealer Moses.

Millions of people have thought with sacred awe that Moses was permitted to negotiate directly with the LORD and therefore must have been divinely elevated in an unparalleled manner.

However, Moses as a religious figure is of only minor significance, even though followers of various faiths might object to this statement. Neither the "laws" that Moses supposedly received from the hand of the LORD and passed on are outstanding original creations of religion, nor do the numerous highly miraculous encounters that this crafty Jewish tribal figure claimed to have had with the LORD awaken anything beyond, perhaps, a psychological interest.

What is exceptionally instructive, however, is the nation-building work of Moses. The fact that the Jews, upon their escape from the Egyptian concentration camp—calling it the Exodus of the Children of Israel is a poetic exaggeration—stole the valuables of their former masters is indeed telling and revealing, but of lesser significance than the actions of the "Angel of Death," that is, a Jewish terror squad that, in the name of the LORD, slaughtered particularly important Egyptian overseers and dignitaries. The LORD wanted the freedom of the Jews, so He gave them victory! This was a very important psychological weapon for combating the last remnants of a slave mentality and marked the first beginning of a "master" attitude, although still tied to Yahweh and therefore lacking true independence.

The LORD wanted the salvation of the Jews, so He miraculously parted the waters of the Red Sea to allow the Jews to pass through on dry land while drowning the Egyptian warriors! Again, a very clever psychological tool to remove the feeling of insecurity from the persecuted and to fill them with the proud confidence: "We are in the hand of the LORD and, through HIM, mightier than the strong!"

This emotional experience of being "stronger than the strong" through "miracles" despite all weakness has remained with the Jews in their entire spiritual life to this very day. All the more shameful is the fact that, to this very day, the spiritual experiences of the Jewish sphere are imposed on the religious souls of foreign races to Judaize these peoples! One only needs to imagine the amusement with which Jews listen to the praise of their Yahweh echoing from cathedrals and churches, monasteries and chapels. They know that Yahweh saved them so that they might be the masters of this earth, to lay the world at the feet of Yahweh. And the very nations whom they are commanded by Yahweh to bring to ruin and death praise HIM, for HE led the Jews through the murderous sea on dry land!

Truly, the Jew can be grateful to his zealous allies, for what once served as a source of spiritual explosive for the preparation of world conquest continued to live on from century to century as a seed of disruption in the souls of "missionized" nations.

What the Jew once proclaimed as the will of the LORD during skillful raids became, in Christianity, missionary campaigns against the souls of still-free nations. The Jew was content to gather treasures on the ruins of nations, while the mission of Christianity does not rest until the last soul is subjected to the "Kingdom of the LORD."

To understand the questions of the "Kingdom of God" and the struggle for its realization, it is necessary to recognize the work of Moses. With great skill, Moses, by presenting Yahweh, the ONE, the LORD, in countless roles, removed from the Jews the feeling of abandonment, of being lost, of being rejected. They were lulled into believing that with Yahweh, they had everything, but without Him, they had nothing.

Are you thirsty, Jew? Behold, you must perish from thirst, for there is no water anywhere! But if Yahweh intervenes at the last moment, you are saved! Just believe, and you will be delivered! And the Jew believes, believes until Moses strikes his staff against the rock, and a fresh spring flows into the sand.

Are you hungry, Jew? Behold, your end is near, for where shall your food come from? Yahweh is your savior, just believe! And Moses lets Yahweh rain manna from heaven!

Do you not know where to set your foot in your hopelessness, Jew? Behold, you must lose your way, you must perish, for there is no escape! But if you believe, Yahweh will take you by the hand and lead you to safety! And Moses lets Yahweh shine ahead of the crowd of Jews in a fiery cloud, guiding them towards a distant but secure destination. And when doubt persists too strongly among the people, Moses lets Yahweh shake the mountains or speak through fire, so that the doubters regain faith: "The Lord is with me; I shall not fear."

Miracle upon miracle follows, and these hammer blows of "revelation" forge the souls into an unbreakable bond with the LORD. Thus, as they are bound to the idea of Yahweh, the Jews become a unity, an unbreakable community of fate.

In later days, prophets arise again and again as smiths to reforge the brittle and fractured parts of this bond.

Moses takes it a step further: he does not just restore a long-lost trust in a—albeit borrowed—strength, he also makes them superior to foreign peoples, as these foreigners have no Yahweh. In spirit, Moses transformed a lost tribe into a people, and to this wandering, deceiving, thieving, murdering people, which represents the dregs of humanity not only racially but especially morally, he gave the right to claim ownership of the entire world with all its riches and values. That is certainly something remarkable!

The Jew clings all the more firmly to the promise of ultimate power, the more he realizes that the moment he lets go of the LORD's hand, he must fall into the abyss. The Jewish religion is fundamentally oriented towards the goal not only of survival but of becoming the ultimate victor and owner of this earth. With his triumph, he is to proclaim the honor of the LORD. This is the only recompense Moses demands.

Yahweh's blessing is manifested in rewarding ways; thus, it would be unwise and suicidal not to be "pious."

The Jew has received this teaching. This was the great work of Moses. Do we now understand why Jewish stories almost exclusively praise the miraculous deeds of Yahweh? The belief must be hardened into a certainty that Yahweh is invincible. From the throne of the LORD, from the Ark of the Covenant, such power emanates that the idols of foreign peoples fall flat when that throne is near.

Weak, small Jewish boys throw down heroes who are not under the blessing of Yahweh with mere pebbles; frail Jewish girls outwit the brave men of foreign nations. Nothing else is meant to be shown but the "salvation fact" that Yahweh is mighty in the weak and elevates him, even when he is clearly in the wrong, above the strong. Therefore, Yahweh prefers a repentant sinner, that is, a sinner who once again submits to his "guidance," over the righteous who do not concern themselves with him.

It is not a matter of right or wrong; it is about who believes in Yahweh. And Yahweh is willing to overlook five faults if one only believes in Him. However, He jealously guards the "true" faith.

An astonishing act that stands almost alone in the intellectual history of humanity, this work of Moses!

One must not forget that the fanatical Jewish horde, under Moses's wise spiritual leadership, despite all distortions and peculiarities, became a people proud of their race, even arrogantly so. We know that the idea of Yahweh is ultimately nothing more than the distorted projection of the rebellious and power-driven instincts of the Jewish soul, as Moses saw and wanted it to be.

In the belief of the Jews, the period of "trials" has always been merely a process of purification, through which the Jewish soul was to be more closely bound to the salvation-bringing Yahweh. Thus, through the intellectual history of Judaism, there runs, up to this very day, that peculiar trait of cold, calculating materialistic cunning and psalm-chanting, almost romantic longing, born from that Mosaic-Yahwist mixture of optimism, opportunism, realism, greed, acquisitiveness, cruelty, gratitude to the benevolent provider Yahweh, lustful destructiveness from a slave's instinct, the communal instinct of the persecuted, the dependency of the weak. This mixture has only grown thicker with the uplifting feeling of being a chosen people reserved for dominion over this earth.

This alone is how the Old Testament can be understood: it is Yahweh's curse upon those who do not heed his command, and the blessing upon those who, under his guidance, choose to unite in an unconditional community.

Merciless toward all that is foreign—spiritually and racially—full of hatred against every strong force, suspicious of every individualistic spirit: so the appointed one of Yahweh, the high priest, jealously watches over the growth of the "godly" state, delighted with anything that serves the ultimate goal, murderous against any, even the most innocent, endeavor to live without Yahweh's influence.

The Jew does not know the pursuit of God, nor does he contemplate ultimate connections, nor does he struggle for the possible understanding of the law: for him, "piety" is obedience to Yahweh. This is the alpha and omega of the entire

Yahwist theology, which grants humanity neither freedom nor exploration, neither truth nor naturalness, but instead drenches it in the will of Yahweh, demanding the sacrifice of any personal growth and banishing the "disobedient."

Any concept of God becomes foolishness before the command of submission. The Old Testament is practically a textbook on the subjugation of souls to a command, a submission to a single will that, as a reward, grants the world.

When the Bible is eventually stripped of its false character as a "religious" book or as a document of the "godly" will for salvation, awakened individuals will stand horrified before the force that once exercised absolute politics on earth under the guise of a "god." Moses, however, will be remembered as an example of a dictator of the soul, the greatest dictator of the soul, who succeeded in raising a people from a restless and wandering horde, tainted with the mark of criminality, by igniting a "religious" will.

The curse of the awakened, however, will fall upon all those who paved the way for Jewish world domination by zealously and self-righteously spreading Jewish "religion" into the world, presumptuously and cruelly, laying the axe to the root of all peoples whose ultimate desire was to live and develop according to their own laws.

Every "world religion" pursues power politics, and even if, as it is said, only two or three gather in the name of their "god," they are so filled with the command of this "god" that they become his tools.

Bibles only exert a magical effect as long as their aura remains fresh. Therefore, they must be renewed and refreshed from time to time. The moment the spell fades and the light of truth, the radiance of the law—which is the only deity—begins to shine through the haze of incense, the strongest awaken from their stupor, the bravest rise from their humility, stand upright, and oppose the source of intoxication.

Then, it becomes very dangerous for the founders of religions to have created "eternal religions."

Indeed, the first to awaken, those who achieve awareness, are endangered because of their understanding. Attempts are made to kill them, ostracize them from their people, or render them "impossible." Yet, their swift actions suffice to tear the blindfolds from the eyes of thousands. These thousands, in turn, bring forth the judgment through which justice attains dominion.

But what are the threats and punishments of those still under the spell of their enslaving "religion" in the face of justice?

The avengers are at the door: just yesterday, the Jews, through their "religion," were on the path to world domination, but today, they flee in fear before the first of the awakened among the nations, seeking the last hiding places on earth.

Yesterday, the enchanted people of all nations knelt before the Jewish patriarchs; today, these peculiar Jewish "saints" are mocked, called frauds, pimps, brazen magicians, and shameless deceivers!

One truth Moses demonstrated: whoever holds the soul of a people or an individual controls all aspects of life—politics, economy, worldview, and longing.

Those who have learned from this "religion" will not rest until they have liberated the soul of their people for truth and action, for reality and law.

"Strengthen the soul of the people!"

For this phrase alone, "world religions" will hate and persecute a man like Ludendorff.

For the realization that race is history and destiny, that world power will never make peace with National Socialism, whose symbol of freedom is the swastika—the sign of creative life, the sun, indivisibility, and the totality of this world.

But what if that world power, that Jewish "religion," collapses? Will not the fearful, lamenting, seek "support" or a purpose in life? Certainly, no one can, wants to, or will give them a "substitute." "Help yourself, and God will help you," demands a harsh but truthful saying.

With Yahweh, the angry and vengeful "God," disappearing, fear vanishes from the world, as does the hope for reward. Thought no longer revolves around those poles; it becomes free for the great demands of this world. The once-humbled man rises to the full greatness of his law and thus to creation, to action. The conscious planting of seeds of life, which he fills with his blood, his spirit, his will, is his action for eternity. And his justice is the work in proper order and his struggle for this order against any arbitrariness.

He who has overcome fear has no need for "hope." For, above all the "hope" of the "servants of God," those who earnestly desire to be subjects, rises the certainty of the strong, that in their knowledge of the law and in their belief in the unchangeable nature of the act leading to perfection lies the eternity of their life struggle.

One who once rose to freedom avoids the snares of redemption religions, which would again lead him into servile dependence, into a subservient relationship with a "God."

The Free, called to mastery over all realities, rejects every "heaven" that would make him submissive, compliant, weak.

The very shrewd Jew Walther Rathenau once revealed in an unguarded moment his knowledge of the conditions of spiritual bondage emanating from Sinai, pointing out that no one could escape Sinai: Moses, Jesus Christ, the liberal philosophy of a Spinoza are, for him, paths leading into the Sinai entanglement!

The Free, who found the way into his own heart, sees the net that invisibly spreads over the entire world.

And does not the one estranged from the church often fall victim to vain sects that bind him even more tightly to Yahweh; does not the one who indulges in spiritualism become a slave to disturbing revelations, which ultimately lead back to the wrathful "God" of Sinai; is not the believer in astrology a will-less victim in the hands of eager "astrologers," who are again marionettes in the hands of certain Jewish-Kabbalistic circles; do not the Theosophists, the Anthroposophists, the Christian Scientists, the Serious Bible Students, the thousands of occult associations and organizations, which seek to lead "humanity" to the "light" through mysteries or even merely through certain "fruit juices," find their master strategists in Sinai; are not, ultimately, all "international" and "supranational" functionaries servants of Sinai, even if they do not want to acknowledge it?

The Free, who has found knowledge and insight, frees himself from all entanglements, even if he is isolated in his freedom. From the mountain of realization, he refuses to be drawn back into the valleys of superstitious and blind fear at any price.

What does it matter to him if the "servants of God" accuse him of godlessness, what does he care if they call him heathen! He laughs at those who label him a destroyer, an unbeliever.

The Free, who affirms the mighty life with its struggles, sufferings, and victories, with its downfalls and ascensions, and who fulfills this life with his action toward perfection, stands above any nihilism, which may characterize the passive.

He who affirms action and seeks its fulfillment already stands above the "void" through his will.

The Free has grown too great in his self-responsibility and too strong in fulfilling his duty to make use of the servile offer: "Call upon me in trouble, and I will rescue you, and you shall glorify me."

The call of the strong is directed solely at his soul, his will, so that resonance may return to his heart, connecting him with the rhythm of the creative law.

The Strong has no need for Yahweh, neither his reward nor his threat. Even patron saints cannot help him, for how else could he be proud of his freedom? However, he greets Prometheus and Lucifer as confidants, as comrades, as fellow travelers toward the perfect homeland of the strong.

Who still dares to pity the strong for his divine defiance?

The magnificent defiance of the Free is more than pride: it is also the great rebellion of instinct against all oppression.

This defiance could also be called the Nordic inherited will to preserve lawful life: for where in the world has defiance filled men's hearts so fully as in the North?

The defiant heart has always been the last refuge in despair in the face of certain death, and the defiant faith in the ultimate victory of the soul over enmity was the last arrow the mortally wounded could shoot.

The heroic songs of the North are at once superior philosophies of defiance, leading men to heights of experience to which no religion can elevate such feelings.

The soul, which in the true man allows that chord to resonate that arises from the harmony of all life-giving forces—blood, will, instinct, spirit—receives through defiance the final lift to an obstacle-overcoming flight, resulting in the mightiest discoveries and the boldest visions.

Thus, Gothic architecture is nothing but the yearning and defiance of Nordic spirituality made stone. And in defiance of narrow dogmatic thinking, the spark of mysticism glowed under the ash of centuries, which was occasionally stirred by the wind of rebellion.

All essential philosophies of modern times, insofar as they were not overshadowed by religions, have struck away the supposedly protective or threatening hand of each respective god of religion in Promethean defiance!

Defiance amplifies yearning into rebellion. Thus, the North was primarily the land of rebels in the truest sense of the word, of those men who rose above the dust of humility and the dependence on foreign powers associated with it, ascending into the free realm of ideas.

Here, the word of the Orient does not apply: "Not as I will, but as you will." Here, the hard demand of the North applies: "What I must do out of duty is also the free will of my heart."

The defiant one scorns those who boast of being prisoners of God, and he delights in his solitude, which places him beyond all servile security.

———

Throughout world history, there have been plenty of defiant individuals who set out as conquerors to impose their will on the world. This will alone deserves the attention of the strong, who are on the lookout for examples and ideas. The successes of the ventures that the defiant and daring once undertook are, compared to the will, of lesser importance. Thus, we today carry within our spiritual inheritance the legacy of the will of our ancestors, even without having historical knowledge of the success of their endeavors. Will demonstrates character and humanity, but never the external success, whose echo in history is all too often distorted.

The North, in its heroic songs—later reflected in the sagas and ballads—rarely inquired about success but always about the will that rises against fate.

People of success can be the greatest perverters of justice and therefore enemies of the law. Exemplary strong individuals, however, will never misuse their power in arbitrary ways, nor will they seek to impose their own law on a foreign humanity.

Where bravery and wisdom unite in the perfection of knowledge of the law, there also reigns the purest humanity, which uses its power to destroy injustice, that is, to bring about the true order of values.

Here, the great rulers separate from the tyrants, and the warriors from the conquerors. Here, too, Lucifer separates from the prophets!

———

Through the concentration of its will and the uprising of its blood, the North has risen again in our days. Its lawful development towards perfection, and thereby towards power, is unfolding unstoppably. Let the weak tremble and plot murder: as long as the North remains strong and knowledgeable within itself, all arrows will be deflected!

Power, however, is the sister of wisdom, and wisdom is nothing other than knowledge of the law. Where the strong violate the law, they stumble, and the end is the downfall of their work and blood.

Ancient Rome perished because its citizens used power to secure a carefree, pensioned existence; but if the grain ships from Africa failed to arrive, hunger, mass unrest, and a weakening of internal and external power ensued.

When one's will grows dull, complacent, and indifferent after achieving external power goals, it dies from the thickening and decay of its blood and proves that its will was corruptible.

The secret to sustaining power lies in the will's ascent to ever-new goals, in the incorruptibility of the idea. Whole, once-healthy nations sank with their unrestrained emperors and kings, whose greed had poisoned their power.

For centuries, the fame of the great Alexander shone across the globe, and countless nations saw in Alexander the ultimate manifestation of human power and glory. He died three hundred years before the turn of the millennium, and it proved that his power was superficial, as it quickly crumbled under the Diadochi.

Nevertheless, Alexander's example is worth studying. Just as the birth of all great and strong figures is bathed in mythical radiance—though the wise distinguish themselves from fools by appreciating myths as myths—a mysterious glow surrounds Alexander's origins. It's known that his father was King Philip and his mother was Olympias, yet legend casts a veil over Alexander's birth. It is said that before her marriage, Olympias dreamed of a great thunderbolt descending from the heavens to wed her, and from her womb emerged a massive ray of fire that spread in all directions before finally fading into the dust.

Thus, Alexander appears before us: a lightning bolt that flames and shines, traverses the world, but ultimately descends into dust—not into the stars. Olympias was a remarkable woman, full of secret desires and daemonic tendencies, a follower of the orgiastic cults of Dionysus. A son begotten by lightning was worthy of her, as was Alexander.

Alexander was the son of such a mother, a mother to whom gods and serpents came! A mother whom even his father admired and feared. It is no coincidence that noble women in the North are visited by gods, and that the sons of these gods are proud of their mothers. Blessed was the blood that shared in the perfection of the gods, consecrated with the noble duty to greatness. So, too, should the maternal women in the land of the strong once again be deemed worthy of giving the bravest men godlike sons, so that a perfected humanity may arise.

Bright fire blazed from Alexander's eyes; his skin was fair, and his hair shone with the radiance of the pale northern sun. Viking blood gave his heart the will to achieve the greatest things and not to be satisfied with small ambitions. And the desire to fulfill his own law made him scorn wealth and all superficialities.

Longing, as only the North knows, granted him the almost supernatural vision of the realm. For him, "realm" embodied the essence of all power, all glory, all expansiveness. He dedicated himself to this vision and this dream, and he remained true to this idea when his father gave him Aristotle as a teacher, who even introduced him to the secret sciences accessible only to a select few.

With grim tenacity, Alexander studied to gain greater knowledge than the men of his time. He is one of the most shining examples that, in addition to strength and bravery, heroes also require knowledge, will, and perseverance.

It was natural for Alexander to yearn to prove his heroism—which is nothing less than fulfilled, knowing humanity. The first tests he passed when his father went to war against Byzantium, acting as the guardian of the Macedonian seal, were convincing: he drove out insurgents and traitors, brought in colonists, and founded the city of Alexandropolis. In the battle of Chaeronea, he fought with outstanding bravery.

Finally, after Philip fell victim to an assassination plot in which Olympias was not entirely innocent, Alexander rose to power. In hard campaigns, he first continued his father's work, the subjugation of Greece. He destroyed Thebes, yet showed mercy towards Athens. With a few decisive actions, he laid the foundations of his future empire: Greece and Macedonia.

From here, he reached for the crown of the world empire. He defeated the Persians for the first time at the Granicus. The Persian Great King Darius III had to retreat step by step, and Alexander took over the vast Persian Empire, the result of centuries of Persian struggles for world domination.

The world lay before Alexander like a rich garden, and treasures seemed to wait for him to claim them: this is the vision that often appears like a mirage before the eyes of many great conquerors, always receding as their victorious sword draws closer to the goal.

However, Alexander surpassed most of his successors in the pursuit of world domination because he personally never gave in to base despotic instincts, never enriched himself, nor focused solely on his own welfare.

Alexander's dream of being the one and true ruler of this world was devoid of greed. Indeed, one could even attribute to Alexander the almost Prussian quality that he served his idea. He felt so deeply destined to fulfill the idea of a world empire that he regretted feeling moments of fatigue and sensual desires, as these reminded him too much of his mortal flesh.

Alexander knew that the strong must overcome all temptations of indulgence, which appear in countless forms to the powerful, in order to remain clear and alert for action. One of his sayings is that it is kingly to live in toil and work, while it is slave-like to surrender to softness and luxury.

These were the spiritual prerequisites with which he created his power! These were the traits of his soul that made him great in the world! He moved forward like a northern god. Nations and kings of the earth bowed before his step, and the treasures of the world lay open to him. He quickly conquered lands as far as the Indus. Then came the collapse.

It is essential to understand the background of this shocking collapse! How could a god die? For the thought that he was the son of a god increasingly dominated his thinking, allowing him to earnestly point to Philip as the steward of his divine father. Alexander eagerly absorbed all philosophies and cults that could justify this divine sonship.

In doing so, he overstepped the natural boundaries set by northern thought on human existence after its perfection. The strong fulfill the law of their lives, become perfect, but never "God." Here, the Orient intervenes, with its belief in the possibility of surpassing humanity and its associated secret doctrines, magic, and superstitious ceremonies, as well as its tangled, miracle-oriented prayer life. When Alexander strayed from the lawful thinking of the North and the philosophies inherent to his nature, he succumbed to the illusion that it was possible to merge incompatible souls, bound by different blood, through a new spiritual direction. This attempt was destined to fail because the soul, as the ultimate, delicate chord of all living inner being, cannot be bent, blended, or transplanted arbitrarily. Experiments with the soul are crimes that exact a bitter toll.

Alexander once attempted to fuse the law of the North with that of the Orient: it was this attempt that led to his failure, this transgression that caused his downfall. His decline began when he introduced the Persian custom of prostration among his Macedonians and had them revere him as a god. At that point, the loyalty of the Macedonians died! Loyalty is a condition of mutual devotion. There is no one-sided loyalty! Alexander became unfaithful, and only a despot could demand "loyalty" while meaning obedience and submission.

The more Alexander adopted the manners and dress of an oriental ruler, the more he lost spiritual harmony with his once-loyal followers. What use was the conquest of the world when he betrayed the loyalty and the faith of the men who had risen with him!

His downfall was profound! Though Alexander adorned himself more splendidly than ever, though his decisions were swifter and more decisive, no longer did a fearless, simple, and hardy Macedonian stand before his soldiers vying for world domination. Instead, he became uncertain, and ultimately fearful and distrustful, of his instruments of power. He could no longer fully trust them because he saw in their hearts the law he had betrayed.

The despot is incapable of loyalty. He can no longer work with living men who stand for duty and honor. The realm he rules over is one of terror and dread.

The strong are kind, generous, and understanding towards those who share their law, yet ruthless to the point of destruction towards their enemies. The despot, however, is equally distrustful and therefore hostile to all those he encounters. The extent of his enmity depends on the potential advantage he might gain from his adversary.

The creatures the despot creates, he destroys as soon as they are no longer useful, as soon as they become bothersome, or possibly even dangerous. The strong make the earth bloom beneath their steps. The despot leaves behind blood, terror, and devastation.

In Alexander's development and actions, one can observe how the light of his character, the constructive and blessing-giving, was gradually overshadowed by the rage, destruction, and cruelty.

Alexander set out to merge the North with the Orient and, in doing so, became an Oriental! A hero traded his fulfilled and perfected humanity for the glittering facade of a crown.

A man abandoned his soul and sank into the oppressive incense-filled atmosphere of an oriental god! The few brave Macedonians who rose, pointed to their scarred chests, cursed the Orient, and desired to return to the North were the loyal, incorruptible ones—the brave men superior to the servile gods.

While Alexander was still able to inspire admiration in his now-silent companions through repeated displays of bravery, he could no longer rekindle their belief in his humanity as being superior to that of the gods. They knew that, as a man, Alexander could be relied upon for anything without disappointment. However, as the god Alexander, he became treacherous, vindictive, and unreliable—just like all gods who have ever offered their assistance to mankind.

What use, then, were Alexander's stirring words that the brave could conquer the world, while even the ground beneath the coward's feet was uncertain? What was the benefit when a courageous philosopher suggested to him in a parable that a king must stand at the heart of his kingdom to preserve it, rather than wandering its farthest edges, lest the balance of power be shifted and lost?

Alexander had become an Oriental. The old Macedonian—the companion of struggle, ascent, power, and glory—had surrendered his place at the king's heart to the young, refined, rested, and elegant Persians. The superior, unwavering stance to which the exhausted, blood-drained Macedonian regiments had once looked with faith had long since left him. The declining Alexander, who had become neither a true man nor a true god, died in fear—a peculiar trait of those caught in-between, who fear the twilight of uncertainty, fate, and death. Did he die of poison? Ancient sources claim so, while others disagree. Either way, it is certain that Alexander was spiritually poisoned, and such poisoning of the soul leads to death faster and more surely than physical poisoning.

Thus ended a man who had set out to victoriously proclaim his law—the law of spiritual Hellenism, the law of the North—to the world. Thus ended a strong and great man who, blinded by power, failed to understand the secret of confining power to his own racial soul—a secret his teacher Aristotle had already revealed to him as a boy.

Many kings and emperors of Nordic blood have perished from the same poison since. Therefore, Alexander's fate is as instructive as his longing and the idea for which he went to war.

Although Alexander was not a "world benefactor" in the modern sense, he was one of those "world improvers" who overlooked the fact that the soul of a race is indivisible and cannot be imparted to nations of other blood, neither as a claim of conquest nor as a religion of salvation.

It took centuries of bitter disappointment and rivers of irreplaceable Nordic blood before the long-buried realization was rediscovered: Only where pure blood gives rise to a harmonious, knowledgeable humanity does the soul find the ultimate harmony of deep life-meaning, the certainty of the law. And the law is indivisible!

The strong, in their homeland, will no longer forget this knowledge! They will find joy in their duty to the nation and will no longer be distracted by utopias that drift in misty realms beyond the life-giving sphere of the nation. In their dedication to the nation, the strong will experience the entire fullness of the world, of becoming, perishing, and renewal: in their homeland lies the world and eternity!

And having a homeland is a deeper happiness than the blessings of the gods of all the earth's religions!

Enticing images and wild longings arise before the souls of the young and strong of the North. Blessed is he who has yearnings! He also has battles that compel him to victory or defeat!

Blessed is he who has the strength to set sail on a swaying ship across raging, roiling seas into the realm of daring and adventure! Only in storms does the seaworthiness of the ship and the bold courage of the helmsman reveal themselves!

But woe to him who sells his yearning for greed and, in doing so, loses the compass that guides him back from adventure to his homeland! He who loses his compass must die and perish, disappearing without a trace into the chaos of lawless drives!

At the end of his torn and aimless life, he may try to reach a new island—one of the many islands of faith that salvation religions offer to their followers as the only rescue from the rushing current of life—to find a new foundation there!

On the rocky shores of these islands lie the weary from life's shipwreck, the disappointed, the defeated! They are easy prey for the soul-catchers who roam with nets and bait!

The homeland of the strong is unshakable land, land with sowing and harvest, with summer and winter. Land of toil and reward.

Land of true security, not of salvation!

Land of fulfillment, never of redemption!

And yet, the flutes of salvation doctrines sound so lovely and seductive that even the strong may be tempted for hours to lay down their swords and follow the mysterious sweet song.

Doesn't it seem true that man is only a guest on earth and that his true homeland is in heaven? Doesn't it sound genuine that all human deeds are in vain before a judging god who values the humble soul of a sick person more than the defiant one of the strong? The flutes of peace can easily have a heart-touching sound that brings tears to the eyes. And images of eternal peace can have a beauty that seems otherworldly! And all too soon, the one who has let his sword sink is met by the caller with his "Follow me!" Through deserts and wastelands goes the path, leading to a barren hill of despair, upon which the tormented, shamed, and broken man allows himself to be nailed to the cursed wood without resistance.

On the way to the hill, the intensity of life fades, giving way to a dull, resigned sorrow. The victorious song of the soul is drowned out by sighs and prayers. But on the hill of despair stands a monument claiming that from here, the path leads to paradise.

———————

The pale prophet of salvation has come to the North. Not himself! But his heralds have sought to carry his soul into the North. It is too late to evade the saving sufferer. He himself calls for battle with his words:

"Whoever is not with me is against me!"

Let it be done to him as he wishes!

The strong hear the call of the Pale One and listen to his story, to make their choice:

if not for him, then against him!

But let the choice be made with a firm heart.

For as the choice is made, so shall homeland and realm be: of this world or of that!

The lord of this world is the strong one who has found a homeland.

This world is there for all who are strong in heart; but who is the lord of that world, which no one can define?

Let us ask the one who has challenged us to this duel!

━━━━━━━━━━━

It is curious to observe that Christianity, gradually developing according to the principles of Jesus of Nazareth, was recognized and rejected by numerous rulers and wise men as a threat to the worldly realm, yet was seldom systematically attacked, despite a strange hesitation often paired with a cautious restraint. Is this restraint rooted in a perhaps understandable human fear of the "divine truths" possibly contained within, making an attack risky? Does Christianity contain some spiritual fortifications that might elevate its followers above their enemies?

Who was Jesus of Nazareth—the Savior, the Messiah, the King of the Jews—that such power could emanate from him?

Was he a god? A prophet? A superhuman? A magician?

Many centuries have pondered this, and many rulers have measured the power revealed in Christianity by the bleeding wounds their people suffered. It is not so much the historical figure of Jesus with his peculiar life story that preoccupies people; rather, it is the mythical Christ and Christianity, named after him, that stirs minds. The Christian principle takes precedence over the personality of Jesus. And the Christian principle began its struggle for power long after the historical Jesus had already been elevated to insignificance in theology compared to the principle itself. There are many who, for whatever reason, lack the courage to confront the truth when they are meant to consider the Christ principle. They prefer to withdraw from this question under the guise of reverence. Yet so-called reverence has never been creative. On the contrary, it has always failed utterly whenever a decisive step was needed to complete the world view! When Christianity launched its revolutionary assault on the old world view, it was anything but reverent! To this day, Christianity showers any intellectual movement that threatens to break from its claim to totality with irreverent accusations and labels! Christianity has had an easy time, as it has always claimed to act "in the name of God" and under his command. Here, the threatening finger of God and his voice, angry out of love; there, the defiant human, the rebel, the "blasphemer!"

However, anyone who believes they can reach the essence of Christianity by examining the historical Jesus and exposing his human fallibility or even the historical inaccuracies of his earthly life will be surprised to find such discoveries utterly fruitless.

The person forced to make a decision quickly leaves the historical plane and disregards Jesus as insignificant in the ultimate matters, instead taking refuge under the cloak of the mythical Christ. And no rational arguments reach that place!

Jesus has always found his Judases, who betrayed him, though this may have been disgraceful betrayal to the historical Jesus; it is called superior strategy when it serves the mythical Christ.

There are Christians—especially from liberal theology—who can make cynical remarks about the historical Jesus and his miracles and "salvific events," yet eagerly defend the Christ principle, even if Jesus no longer belongs to it. This is a peculiar condition that the non-theologian rarely understands. And the theologian, in turn, is usually cautious not to reveal too much about their Christology, as flexible as any syncretistic philosophy!

Jesus of Nazareth and Christ, the Resurrected and Exalted, are two principles that need not agree any more than the theology of Paul with that of Peter, the theories of justification of Anselm of Canterbury with those of Schleiermacher, or the meditations of Francis of Assisi with those of Karl Barth! Some theologians take interest in the "history of salvation" only after the crucifixion of their religious founder, while others would joyfully sacrifice themselves for the historical truth that Jesus of Nazareth walked on water.

The fact that the Jesus-Christ image is anything but unified has not led Christian believers to distance themselves from it. On the contrary, this very disunity has spawned countless fanatical, exclusivist sects. And whenever disputes among churches and sects appeared to reach a point of fatigue or resignation, a new apostle would appear in time to introduce a new interpretation, causing further confusion and renewed fanaticism.

Common sense cannot unravel the tangible spiritual and ecclesiastical wanderings; Christianity is, after all, a "religion!" And in the force field of "religion," all natural laws are suspended. The priest is rightly the closest relative of the magician, the sorcerer—only the sorcerer is far more vulnerable, as he faces the threat of legal persecution!

In the image of Jesus Christ that has come down to us today, two concepts are combined:

Firstly, the concept of the historical Jesus of Nazareth, the Messiah and King of the Jews, who was crucified.

Secondly, the myth of the Son of God, the second Adam, the creator of a new humanity, the beginning of a new, redeemed mankind.

As these two ideas became more intertwined, theologians emerged!

When theologians gained power over souls, churches arose!

As the churches absorbed numerous other beliefs and notions into their structure, sects emerged from disputes over "truth."

Anyone who wishes to trace the path of Christianity must return to its origins and not believe that analyzing the existing churches will bring clarity. The churches are manifestations of theological, power-driven world schemes. Therefore, theology itself must be examined with respect to the Christian principle!

The path of the historical Jesus of Nazareth is short and of little significance. As is well known, Judaism awaited its Messiah, who was supposed to lead it to world domination by the safest means possible. Yahweh had promised to give the nations to Israel to consume! The prophets had urged Jews before their often brutal ends to remain loyal to Yahweh and not abandon His plans. The prophecy culminated in the promise that the time was near when Yahweh's ultimate dominion over the entire earth would commence. The anointed one of the Lord would lead the charge. (The story of the walls of Jericho collapsing is a suggestion of how simply—through sheer fear of Yahweh—the Jews envisioned the conquest of the world. The Messiah was not a warrior but "Immanuel," the Prince of Peace, whose "peace," however, was to begin only after all peoples were subdued under Sinai. So even today, the beginning of the "Kingdom of God" is synonymous with the "conversion" of the last "heathen.")

"He shall rule from sea to sea and from the river to the ends of the earth. Before him, those in the desert shall bow, and his enemies will lick the dust. The kings by the sea and on the islands shall bring gifts.

The kings from the land of Arabia and Sheba shall offer gifts.

All kings will worship him, and all nations will serve him."

The concept of the Messiah is typically Jewish. Imperialism is made more exclusive, more persuasive, and—safer—through invoking the Lord God! A great sense of expectation of ultimate victory accompanied the idea of the Messiah throughout the history of Israel. And into this history, the historical Jesus saw himself placed!

"Therefore I will give him a great multitude as spoil, and he shall have the strong as plunder, because he gave his life unto death and was counted among the criminals, though he bore the sins of many and interceded for the transgressors."

The historical Jesus is nonsensical without the role of Messiah, and the Messiah, in turn, is inconceivable without his connection to Judaism. "Prophecy" in theology refers to the Old Testament, which gains its significance as a preparation for the Messiah (without this significance, theology would have to dismiss the Old Testament as purely a Jewish matter, but no knowledgeable theologian seriously considers that!). The New Testament, on the other hand, is regarded as the "fulfillment." Jesus cannot be separated from the Jewish foundation of doctrine and claim—without it, his messianic identity would collapse! And without this title, which alone dares to demand humanity's obedience, what would Jesus, the son of Mary, have to say?

The Gospels have only one final purpose: to prove Jesus as the Messiah.

"A redeemer will come to Zion, to those who repent from transgression in Jacob."

This Messiah, and no other, was awaited by Judah, and this Messiah was seen in Jesus by his followers. This is the image that runs through the entire Bible as longing and fulfillment—who would want to deny Judah this Messiah?

"Say to the daughter of Zion, behold, your salvation is coming, and his reward is with him, and his vengeance is before him."

"In those days, Judah shall be saved and Israel shall dwell safely. And this shall be his name, which shall be called, 'The Lord is our righteousness.'"

"In the days of these kingdoms, the Lord of Heaven will establish a kingdom that will never be destroyed and whose rule shall not be passed to another people. It shall crush all those kingdoms and stand forever."

"Soon the Lord whom you seek shall come to his temple, and the angel of the covenant whom you desire."

"I know that the Messiah is coming, whom they call Christ; when he comes, he will reveal everything to us." Jesus answered the woman, "I who speak to you am he."

The certainty of faith in Judaism revolved around the Messiah, without whom suffering would have been meaningless! For the sake of the founding of the messianic kingdom, Judah felt itself uplifted and redeemed from every downfall and deepest despair until the "Day of Judgment," the day of Yahweh's kingdom.

Paul says in the letter to the Romans:

"...for they are Israelites, to whom belong the adoption, the glory, the covenants, the lawgiving, the worship, and the promises; to whom the patriarchs belong, and from whose lineage the Messiah came in the flesh."

To fulfill his role as Messiah, the historical Jesus must carry the proof of "scripture," of prophecy. He must be the King of the Jews, the son of Yahweh. Yes, he must even demonstrate magical power, just as Moses had to perform miracles to convince his Jewish comrades that he was a confidant of Yahweh! Jesus must be a miracle worker, or no one would believe him capable of the Messiah's role! Jesus' recruitment of followers is veiled with miraculous acts. In this, he initially differs little from the typical Jewish prophets, who always sought to draw the attention of their kin through miraculous acts or peculiar messages, striking attire (to the point of offensiveness), or a pronounced world-weariness. This approach is used by the majority of sects that proudly consider themselves part of the spiritual Israel to this day.

Traditional Judaism placed great importance on a continuous genealogy, so Jesus—or those advocating his messianic legitimacy—must point to his descent from Abraham, must present himself as a descendant of the mythical King David of Judah. Even Joseph, who, in a celibate marriage—hence the "Joseph marriage"—with Mary, was not involved in the conception of Jesus, is included in the genealogy as proof of Jesus's Jewish bloodline. This reveals the care taken to establish proof of Jesus's pure Jewish heritage. Here, it is a matter of "insurance," in case the argument of the Holy Spirit is rejected.

The Messiah of the Jews must be fully Jewish! Therefore, it is self-evident that he is circumcised in his youth, marking him as a member of Yahweh's covenant. The cult surrounding Jesus' foreskin, maintained by the church to this day, is characteristic of the deliberate continuation of Yahweh's covenant in Christianity. Equally significant is that the Pope and the chief rabbi bestow upon each other the Aaronic blessing, which begins with "The Lord bless you and keep you"—an essential part of Christian worship.

The main task of the original apostles was to relate all the prophets from Samuel onwards to the historical Jesus. They even went so far as to interpret the entire history of Israel as the revelation field of Yahweh in Jesus Christ.

It is self-evident that the God of the historical Jesus is the Yahweh of the Old Testament: "Think not that I have come to abolish the law or the prophets. I have not come to abolish but to fulfill!"

Just as the church cannot be separated from Christianity, Jesus cannot be removed from the Old Testament. One can try reading the New Testament without the foundation of the Old Testament or attempting to understand the will of the New Testament's God without Yahweh's words, miracles, and promises—but to no avail!

The adversary of Yahweh, according to Jesus, is Satan. Jesus feels compelled to destroy Satan's kingdom to establish Yahweh's kingdom and its final rule: "But if I drive out demons by the Spirit of God, then the kingdom of God has come upon you. Or how can anyone enter a strong man's house and plunder his possessions without first tying up the strong man? Only then can he plunder his house."

"The Son of God appeared for this purpose, to destroy the works of the devil."

Notably, everything that does not come from Yahweh is from the devil! This is a distinctly Jewish perspective.

"Now judgment is upon this world; now the ruler of this world will be cast out."

To redeem Israel, the Messiah must first set out to defeat Satan, who embodies all power that stands against Israel's claim to world dominion. "Satan stood against Israel!"

At no moment did the historical Jesus distance himself from his homeland, Judaism. He considered himself called to lead the lost sheep of Israel into the grace pastures of Yahweh. With particular emphasis, the childhood story of Jesus is addressed in the Gospels to show the Jews that the Messiah came from a genuinely Jewish environment. Mary and Joseph bring the child Jesus to Jerusalem to dedicate him to Yahweh, as prescribed by the law of Moses for firstborn sons.

Only a young Jew from such a family, who has received his religion from the Old Testament, could later stand in the temple as though it were the house of his Father! A future time will no longer understand why there could have been disputes over such self-evident matters. People will come to recognize Jesus as the greatest proponent of an imperialistic Judaism—a Judaism that, because it claimed spiritual and emotional totality, was capable of becoming a world religion.

Today, however, thanks to theologians and pseudo-scientists, a mythical veil has been meticulously placed over the image of Jesus, enabling any fantasy and even falsification. The Jewish Jesus stands in the synagogue and preaches to Jews! The Jewish Jesus gathers Jewish disciples! Jesus, the Jew, stands in the Jewish temple and fights as a member of a radical Jewish baptismal sect (baptized by a Jew, John) for a purified, penitent Yahweh faith.

To his Jewish disciples, Jesus the Jew could say: "Do not go on the road of the Gentiles, and do not enter any city of the Samaritans; go rather to the lost sheep of the house of Israel. Proclaim as you go, saying, 'The kingdom of heaven is at hand.'" The King of Heaven, however, is Yahweh, and no one else! And the envoy of this King Yahweh is Jesus! The herald of the ruthless King Yahweh, who wants to make the nations bow and place them as a footstool at his feet, who wants to make the queens of nations nurses for the Jewish children, who wants to give the Jews the flesh of the strong to eat and the blood of the princes to drink, is the historical Jesus!

If only this conceptual confusion would end, and a clear division of spirits could take place! The fight for the freedom of the soul, and thus for the homeland of the strong, would be much easier!

Jesus as the miracle worker, to whom wind and sea obey; as the prophetic seer, to whom the future is revealed; as the sorcerer who banishes demons into swine, is a Jew of purest Jewish thought, which appears in occult Christian writings as well as in purely Jewish Kabbalah.

Never could an Aryan, even with the best intentions, immerse himself in the Jewish tradition, for this Jewish tradition has always been sealed to those of foreign races. Now, however, people arise who wage the hopeless struggle for a retroactive Aryanization of Jesus of the House of David, claiming that Jesus was crucified due to his "anti-Semitism"!

Hardly any Jewish prophet died a natural death, so the crucifixion of Jesus is nothing extraordinary! Rather, Jesus had to die because he did not immediately visibly fulfill the messianic expectations of law-abiding Judaism. Judah expected the Messiah to immediately subjugate the world. Jesus indeed proclaimed the imminent establishment of that final kingdom, but without being the one to establish it himself. For that reason, they tore the messianic mantle from his shoulders. Thus they cried "Crucify him" where they had just cried "Blessed be he."

The reasons for the crucifixion are purely intra-Jewish in nature. This was also understood by the pagan men who were tasked with settling the Jews' dispute with Jesus.

Only after the death of Jesus was his teaching carried out beyond the walls of Jerusalem to the "Gentiles." To establish the baptism of Gentiles, it required a particularly uncomfortable miracle for a Jew at Joppa, where a large sheet filled with various "unclean" animals was lowered from heaven, and the voice of the Lord called to Peter, telling him to eat these animals. Eating the unclean animals meant nothing other than the admission of non-Jews into the covenant of the Jewish Christians! This was a truly unequivocal commentary on Yahweh's word regarding the gathering of nations and an interpretation of Jesus' statement about the yeast that was to leaven the world. Paul also had to realize this later, when he saw on the road to Damascus that Jesus was not the end of Judaism, but rather the messianic beginning of a new, elevated, more spiritually effective Judaism.

The Messiah Jesus shifted his message from the realm of real power to the realm of spiritual power. In doing so, he gave Israel a completely new face. And from the Jewish claim arose the radical religion with the demand for salvation for all nations, to submit in "faith" and thus also in flesh.

Unfortunately, knowledge of the historical Jesus has been so far pushed into the background in favor of the mythical Christ that the Jewish root has been almost obscured. And theologians have done everything possible to prevent any clarity from emerging in the fog of Christologies and teachings of Jesus.

The confused coexistence and intermingling were more favorable to "religion," as the mystical fog and the opaque emotional world are particularly suited to giving people that peculiar mood in their hearts that suppresses thought and will, fostering a comforting sense of "being sheltered."

This is fully achieved when sinking into the mythical Christ, the mysterious, supernatural Son of God, who is omnipresent and active in helping, healing, redeeming, and comforting. Hardly a more beautiful comfort exists on earth for the weak and forsaken than the certainty of being in the salvific proximity of Christ, the grace-channel of the divine Father.

If the historical Jesus, the miracle worker, could lead minds into the anxieties and hopes of occultism, then the mythical Christ is practically the herald of the "other world," the better, mystery-filled, spirit-laden world to which reason has no key and can only be opened by the magic wand of willing, surrendering faith.

If the historical Jesus arose from the Jewish messianic longing, the mythical Christ arises from the need for redemption of all the weak, the desperate, the incapable of life, and—from the spiritual cunning of theologians! For one realization should be stated upfront: the mythical Christ is solely a construction of theology. This construction goes so far that Christ becomes a principle for whose sake the historical Jesus never even needed to have existed if he were not required to harden this idea!

Into the mythical Christ was poured everything that was present in the spiritually charged and idea-laden atmosphere of the Hellenistic decline in the Mediterranean world. Here, imagination could roam freely, logic could take grotesque leaps, and, if necessary, the most blatant charlatanry could emerge! In the realm of "faith," there are no truths that can be measured by the standards of intellect, reason, or instinct. For this reason, Christianity as a religion could promise anything to anyone: it had an enormous capacity for spiritual expansion, easily encompassing even the most glaring contradictions.

The New Testament is already full of reefs and contradictions, and the so-called Pauline letters stand in the greatest conceivable opposition to the Gospels. Furthermore, the original writings of the so-called "Apostolic Fathers," which were not included in the Bible, now appear in a nearly comical light. Theology knows very well why countless "Gospels," revelations, and letters had to disappear over the centuries instead of being canonized and included in the Bible! These eliminated Gospels also referred to Jesus Christ in his duality but, like the letters of the Apostolic Fathers, were so burdensome for the intellect that they were discreetly set aside, much like the utterances of certain mentally uninspired but exceptionally pious Church Fathers.

Even today, the Church has an exceedingly broad conscience in matters of spirituality, capable of incorporating entire "pagan" customs, only to label them as purely Christian practices once digested.

In the history of early Christianity and the developing Church, the theory of the mythical Christ was the great bag into which everything growing and flourishing along the way was gathered. Simon the Magician, Paul of Tarsus, rabbis, storytellers found a place alongside Plato and Philo, just as, later, under Louis the Pious, the "Savior" was allowed to don a Germanic garment! Indeed, it is easy to say that the Bible has answers to all questions! And it is even easier to say that here "neither Greek nor Roman matters."

And because theology has always shrewdly forbidden itself from being measured by the philosophical standards of critical knowledge, it was able to maintain a highly demanding and costly separate existence. Who would seriously evaluate the Bible as a book of intellect? Who would even seek confirmation of particular scientific truths within it? Or would anyone seriously claim that the Bible is historically accurate or reliable to even the slightest degree?

There is no real truth in the Bible! No truth one would need to confront with force and struggle!

There are only "parables" that demand interpretation, and each interpretation generates new fog.

Indeed, one cannot wrestle with the "kindness" and friendliness of the mythical Christ; it smiles forgivingly and enigmatically but remains—silent! This has been the great weapon of the "faithful" up to this day: they know how to use the shield of "kindness" to conceal their complete intellectual nakedness!

The more the Jewish Messianism of Jesus developed into the religion of Christianity, the more the mythical Christ moved into the center of attention. The Messiah, who was to come to prepare the kingdom of the King Yahweh, was gradually overshadowed by the Christ, who intended to bring redemption from the sins of this world—though still with the ultimate aim of establishing the kingdom of God!

Jewish-Christian theology constructed the following idea: the first creation fell through Adam. The original sin was the desire to be like God, meaning the desire to understand the laws governing life. From this arose the fall into historicity. The woman is the stimulus of sin; she carries the seed of life, and her womb bears the original sin that affects every child born under the sinful law of procreation. Every procreation is a new fall from grace, every birth completed original sin.

Had Adam not allowed sin entry through Eve, paradise would never have been lost. Then there would have been no life on earth, which is toil and labor under Yahweh's curse. Only a second Adam, the initiator of a second humanity, could bring redemption from the curse-law of the first humanity! This second Adam must stand beyond the curse-law; he must be free from "original sin" and thus cannot have a fleshly father.

From this strange line of thought of early Christian theologians arose the even stranger assertion that Christ was conceived by the Holy Spirit in a completely untouched, "immaculate" virgin.

The fact that this claim of "sinless" conception turns all laws on their heads does not trouble theology, for it represents the interests of a "religion," and there, reason must remain forever silent. It is amusing to witness how, in defending even the most absurd theses, theologians raise a finger, furrow their brows, and murmur mysteriously that God's ways are indeed marvelous and not human ways! Reason must bow before the miracle! But when reason and knowledge of the law attempt, in the name of worldly truth, to put an end to the most outrageous theses, theologians cry that God has been blasphemed! How theologians know this, however, remains their divine secret.

The second Adam, then, is fundamentally removed from all earthly traits and thus from any possibility of sinning. This extends so far that he is quickly elevated as the "Logos" into the creative will of Yahweh, where he is entirely secure. And in the system of the Trinity, which theology acquired as dogma after extremely heavy and costly struggles, Christ can no longer be separated from the three-core fruit of God. This anchoring of the religious founder in the concept of God as a world religion is indeed unique and dramatically illuminates Christianity's claim that its faith is infinitely more than one of many religions!

To redeem Israel, the Messiah must first set out to defeat Satan, who embodies all power that opposes Israel's claim to world domination.

"The Satan stood against Israel!"

Not for a moment did the historical Jesus abandon his homeland, Judaism. He felt called to bring the lost sheep of Israel into Yahweh's pasture of grace.

For this reason, the childhood story of Jesus is treated with particular affection in the Gospels, to show the Jews that the Messiah came from an authentic Jewish background. Mary and Joseph bring the child Jesus to Jerusalem to consecrate him to Yahweh, as the Mosaic law prescribes for firstborn sons.

Only a young Jew from such a family, who received his religion from the Old

Testament, could later stand in the temple as if it were the house of his Father!

A later era will no longer understand why such obvious things could be disputed. People will come to recognize Jesus as the greatest proponent of an imperialistic Judaism, a Judaism that, because it claimed total spiritual and emotional dominance, was capable of becoming a world religion!

But today, thoroughly disguised by theologians and pseudoscientists, a mythical veil covers the image of Jesus, allowing for any imagination and any fabrication.

The Jewish Jesus stands up in the synagogue and preaches to Jews!

The Jewish Jesus gains Jewish disciples!

Jesus, the Jew, stands in the Jewish temple and fights as a member of a radical Jewish baptist sect (baptized by a Jew named John) for a purified, repentant Yahweh-faith!

To his Jewish disciples, Jesus, the Jew, can say:

"Do not go onto the paths of the Gentiles, and do not enter any city of the Samaritans; rather, go to the lost sheep of the house of Israel, and proclaim as you go that the kingdom of heaven is near!"

But the King of Heaven is Yahweh, and no one else!

And the envoy of this King Yahweh is Jesus!

The forerunner of the fierce King Yahweh, who wants to subjugate nations and make them a footstool, who will make queens of nations the wet nurses of Jewish children, who will give the Jews the flesh of the strong to eat and the blood of princes to drink, is the historical Jesus!

If only this confusion of concepts would finally end and a true separation of spirits would take place! The fight for the freedom of the soul and thus for the homeland of the strong would be much easier!

Jesus, as the miracle worker whom the winds and seas obey, as the prophet with foresight, as the magician who banishes demons into swine, is a Jew of the purest Jewish mindset, which is evident in both occult Christian writings and the purely Jewish Kabbalah!

Never could an Aryan, even with the best intentions, immerse himself in

Jewish tradition, for this Jewish tradition has always been sealed to those of other races.

And now people have arisen who undertake the hopeless task of retroactively "Aryanizing" Jesus from the house of David, claiming that Jesus was crucified because of his "antisemitism"!

Hardly any Jewish prophet died a natural death, so the crucifixion of Jesus is nothing extraordinary! Rather, Jesus had to die because he did not visibly fulfill the messianic expectations of law-abiding Judaism immediately! Judea expected the Messiah to achieve immediate world conquest. Jesus, while proclaiming the imminent establishment of this final kingdom, was not himself the enforcer. Thus, the messianic mantle was stripped from his shoulders. Thus, they shouted "Crucify him," where they had just shouted "Blessed be he."

The reasons for the crucifixion are purely internal to Judaism. The pagan men tasked with settling the Jews' case against Jesus recognized this as well.

Only after the death of Jesus was his teaching carried outside the walls of Jerusalem to the "Gentiles." To enforce the baptism of the Gentiles, a most embarrassing miracle was required at Joppa, where a large sheet containing all sorts of "unclean" animals descended from heaven, and the voice of the Lord called to Peter, commanding him to eat these animals. For the eating of unclean animals meant nothing other than the admission of non-Jews into the community of Jewish Christians! This was a truly unequivocal commentary on Yahweh's promise of gathering the nations and an interpretation of Jesus's words about the leaven that would leaven the whole world. Later, Paul also had to recognize this when he realized on the road to Damascus that Jesus was not the end of Judaism but rather the messianic beginning of a new, elevated, spiritually more effective Judaism!

The Messiah Jesus shifted his message from the realm of real power to the realm of spiritual power. Thus, he gave Israel a completely new face. And from the Jewish claim arose a radical religion with the demand for salvation for all nations, requiring submission in "faith" and thus also in flesh.

Unfortunately, the knowledge of the historical Jesus has been pushed so far back in favor of the mythical Christ that the Jewish roots have almost been covered over. And theologians did everything they could to prevent any clarity from piercing the fog of Christologies and teachings about Jesus.

The confusing coexistence and mixture were more advantageous for "religion," as the mystical fog and the opaque emotional world are particularly suited to giving people that peculiar mood which shuts down thinking and will, creating a cozy feeling of "security."

This feeling is fully achieved by immersing oneself in the mythical Christ, the mysterious, otherworldly Son of God, who can be present everywhere, helping, healing, redeeming, and comforting. On Earth, there seems to be hardly a more beautiful comfort for the weak and the abandoned than the certainty of being in the proximity of Christ's salvation, the mercy-gate of the divine Father!

If the historical Jesus was the miracle worker who could lead minds into the fears and hopes of occultism, the mythical Christ is practically the messenger of the "other world," the better, mystery-filled, spirit-laden world that reason cannot access, which can only be opened with the magic wand of willing, yielding faith.

If the historical Jesus sprang from the Jewish messianic longing, the mythical Christ emerges from the need for redemption felt by all who are weak, desperate, incapable of life—and from the spiritual cunning of theologians! For let this be stated in advance: the mythical Christ is solely the construction of theology. This construction goes so far that Christ becomes a principle for which the historical Jesus never needed to have lived, had he not been needed to solidify this idea.

The prophets, who stirred the original instincts of vengeance among their kinfolk, could at most lead their followers into wars. The historical Jesus awakened in his disciples the capacity for suffering. The mythical Christ demands from his followers complete passivity, that is, to become vessels of Yahweh's will:

"Not as I will, but as you will!"

Humans are either instruments upon which the Spirit of the LORD plays or containers in which Satan rages!

Whoever truly commits to transformation emulates Christ! They forgive, share, pray, refrain from bearing children, do not take up the sword, and await the day of the LORD.

The early Christian community lived with the desire to transform in the light of the mythical Christ.

"Neither man nor woman!" Thus, they attempted, albeit unsuccessfully, to live without gender distinctions in communal houses.

"Sell what you have." Thus, they freed themselves from wealth and lived in communal societies. Any transgression against this communal ideal was punished by the Holy Spirit with death.

"Faithfulness to Yahweh!" Thus, the (possibly antisemitic?) Jewish Christians went daily to the Temple and adhered to the Jewish ritual laws.

"Put your sword away!" Thus, the Christians offered no resistance anywhere, demonstrating an extraordinary pacifism!

"All people are equal before God!" Therefore, Jewish Christians could confidently break the racial principle and accept tax collectors and Gentiles among them, baptizing them and thereby making them — into Jews!

From this early community, Christianity gradually emerged as a world power. For the sake of their religion, this world power deprived the strong, who did not possess humility as a prerequisite for salvation, of their homeland!

After the pitiful bankruptcy of early Christianity, there is no true Christianity left, but there is still a Christian principle, and that is the claim of the weak to rule for the sake of "faith." In the papacy, which inherited the legacy of the Roman Empire, this principle became political power. This principle has spawned all democracies and sanctioned all slave revolts. It has persecuted the strong and murdered the solitary. It has hollowed out nations and mixed races.

———————————

"What do you think of Christ?" asks the suspicious voice of the "other" world.

We have given our answer, my friends.

We had to take a long, winding path of thought to outline the contours of the double-faced image of Jesus Christ.

Often, anger has overtaken us, for the blood shed by men of the North for the kingship of Yahweh!

But we have walked this path to its end, to remove the mythical veil and to reveal that it was not an Aryan hero who walked upon the waters of the Sea of Galilee nearly two thousand years ago, but rather an ordinary Jewish prophet around whom an entire ideological structure has been built, reaching into the highest heavens.

In our flight, we have followed the construction of this Messiah-Christ world empire and, through insight, have become aware that we will not be caught in the net of these "fishers of men."

Because we have set out to have a homeland, we renounce citizenship in Yahweh's kingdom.

Glorious defiance bids us walk past the temples where the masses who call themselves sheep are gathered, with heads held high. Yes, we rejoice that we have no reverence for the mental constructs of pilgrims who seek to build bridges from this world of truth to that other world of assertion.

Because we love the nation, which is to become our homeland, we have no reverence for structures that would block out our German heaven. We are too devout in our own law to be "neutral"! Perhaps we lack an "organ" for the faith of that other world;

Certainly, we do not have it! For all our senses and desires belong to this world, which is the homeland of the nation, the mother of all our longings.

No one shall take us by the hand to lead us to Yahweh, where the Jewish patriarchs, prophets, and messiahs sit; we want to remain in Germany!

Our victory songs may be wilder and more fervent, but they are also more heartfelt and sincere than the monotonous sighs of medieval sourpusses!

Both the historical Jesus and the mythical Christ have challenged us.

"Whoever is not for me is against me!"

We are firmly opposed to them!

We do not fear hell!

What is Yahweh's paradise to us compared to the heart of Germany?

Let us find this heart and have a homeland, while others think we have gone to hell!

Let us return the Bible of the "pious" to the Jews; after all, they also have no use for the heroic songs of the North!

What are the joys of heaven, what is the peace of the blessed, compared to the struggle of homeland and the yearning of the strong;

"Our soul is in danger," say the "others."

Let us answer that we love danger, daring, commitment, courage, and — freedom!

The work of the pale Messiah and the Christ elevated to Yahweh lies beyond the sphere where the strong breathe and live.

When the hallelujahs echo from there, the strong do not plug their ears but instead raise their victorious songs.

They do not divide their possessions to follow the pale one but tighten their swords and press the plow deeper into their native soil.

Since their will has awakened, they are careful not to be "redeemed." They know that the "other" world must destroy their homeland to establish Yahweh's kingdom; therefore, they do not grow complacent in their vigilance but instead forge the weapons of knowledge.

The son of Yahweh intends to return to pass judgment! Like a thief in the night, he plans to come!

Thus, the careless may think he has long since died.

But the strong know that Christ lives as an idea and acknowledges nothing but itself: Therefore, the strong will never lay down their sword!

Countless are the voices of powers and men who appeal to the longings of the young.

Countless are the temptations and promises, the pleas and threats, so that the young must steel their hearts to avoid straying from the path of understanding the law.

The most famous men in the world are not always the most heroic examples of a strong and law-abiding life.

Therefore, those who yearn should recognize early on that external success, conquest, is not the hallmark of a valid life, but rather that only inner loyalty and duty determine it. Duty is incompatible with an imperialism that ends in arbitrariness.

The greatness of an example is measured by the kind of longings it instills in the hearts of seekers.

And the longings a great figure leaves behind attest to his superiority and uniqueness, not by how many happily secured people mourn his passing!

When the young travel to the grave of a great person to feel his spirit, that is his true immortality. In comparison, emperors and kings appear small who merely sought to provide their subjects with a chicken in every pot. The small happiness of well-being is as quickly mortal as a whim; only the great happiness of a role model, which lives on in men and their work, is immortal.

To the North, due to its inherent laws, imperialism is foreign. A deeply agrarian people, a people conscious of its blood, understands the dangers of mixing in foreign environments. It avoids these dangers alone, while viewing all other risks as tests of courage and capability.

On the other hand, imperialism is inherently ingrained in nomads, who have therefore produced the greatest imperialists. Where nomadic races preserved their bloodline and took pride in their race, they practiced a militant form of imperialism that, in its achievements, was often admirable.

The purest nomadic races are those of Central Asia; from there came brave warriors who spread across the world.

The most abhorrent nomadic races are among the Semitic peoples, whose most degenerate group, the Jewish people, engages in the basest form of imperialism—the imperialism of the merchant, which requires no courage, only cunning.

The imperialists who emerged from Europe were often marked by a nomadic disposition, as exemplified by Napoleon.

They nearly all had the greed but seldom the fanatic courage and blood-conscious conviction of their mission, as did the great nomadic leaders of Central Asia.

We regard Genghis Khan, the Mongol, as the greatest nomadic leader of distant Asia, who nearly eight hundred years ago broke down his leather tents to become the ruler of the world.

This Mongol is a remarkable example of the enormity of a will to power, which can fill a person so completely that body and soul become mere instruments of a singular will!

The will of Genghis Khan was of such wildness that it could lead to indescribable acts of cruelty; however, his will never tolerated cruelty as an end in itself. Rather, it repeatedly pulled the soul away from instinctual urges and led it to the pure heights of an ideal!

Anyone who wishes to understand the imperialistic potential dormant within the Mongol race must study and comprehend the work of Genghis Khan. This imperialism stands at the gates of Europe; it resides in the steppes of Russia as well as in the vast expanse of Mongolia. And everywhere a drop of steppe blood reaches, the ambition for world domination germinates. The Near East, too, bears steppe blood!

It is said that Genghis Khan had fair hair and bluish eyes! Yet, his inner disposition was purely Mongolian. His longing was born from the fires of the steppe, over which stretched an infinitely wide sky. A disdain for confinement and its people was ingrained in his nomadic soul.

With mare's milk, he absorbed the desire to roam and to storm, so that he became one with the horses even inwardly. His first conscious cry in life was hatred and vengeance against the enemies of his clan, against the murderers of his father, against the robbers of his property.

Genghis Khan was poor in possessions during his youth, but rich in schemes, in cunning, in aspirations, in hatred, and in enmities! With a tenacity almost unique to the Mongol, he hardened his body until it became as flexible as a bowstring, from which the will could shoot the arrow of longing. And wherever that arrow landed, Genghis Khan rode and took possession of his inheritance.

He was enough of a warrior to know that only the few, the perfected, through the concentration of their will, are able to lead masses into victorious campaigns. Therefore, he won the bravest as friends by proving himself braver than the bravest and becoming a role model for the best. The selection of the perfected shone through their example and convinced the young, who flocked to Genghis Khan.

This way, he was able to begin uniting the Mongols, who, scattered across the vast lands, were subjects to many tribal leaders, into a single people. And he filled this people with the fanaticism of belief in the mission of their race and its dominion, so that ultimately, the Mongol people—after the inner dissenters had been killed or scattered—obeyed a single will as one body.

Take note: a man found his law and sought out the best of his blood for the alliance of the perfected! This alliance became the core people, the secret heart that soon circulated blood through the entire nation.

The core people remained as the carriers of the hardest will to dominion even after the Mongols became a unified people, just as the perfected, as bearers of the rising state's power, could not simply dissolve into the masses.

This united will—the unity of individual insight, the knowledge of the perfected, the loyalty of the core people, and the obedience of the Mongol masses—allowed Genghis Khan to hurl himself like a lightning bolt into a world that was decaying and fragmented.

Even after he rose to power, he never forgot that the structure of his empire would shatter if he were to remove the core people or, worse, the perfected—the very supports of the entire structure. The secret of Genghis Khan's sustained power lay in his personal policies, always placing the right man in the right place. The right man was given full authority necessary for the exercise of total rulership. To betray Genghis Khan was, moreover, an act of suicide, for the Khan's power stretched across the entire earth, and the world was too small to hide a traitor. And what could the unfaithful hope to gain through betrayal? The Khan could give them everything, even the head of any enemy who had offered bribes.

In the knowledge that he had the loyalty of the men he led and who were unconditionally dedicated to his goals, Genghis Khan could undertake the most dangerous ventures with confidence. His men were so steeped in the Mongol law that they undertook any required act, knowing the importance of its swift execution.

Above all, the Khan understood that the individual only has meaning in relation to the community: he demanded from his perfected ones a radiant and inspiring example! The perfected had to live a far harder and more dangerous life than the masses. Thus, over the long campaigns, an aristocracy emerged, hard and incorruptible enough to remain faithful and execute the will of the Mongol race embodied in Genghis Khan, even in isolated and unobserved posts.

This is precisely what made the Mongols appear as "demons" to the spiritually fragmented and thus directionless Europe, both internally and externally. The Asian ferocity intensified this image to that of devilish grimaces. The blood of slain enemies literally dripped from their hands, for the Mongols killed anything that could later pose a threat. The women of other races were often spared, however, as they knew that concentrated Mongol blood could overpower and absorb the already fading blood of the West.

The value of the destroyed cultures, the blood of the fallen, all the atrocities committed by the murderous and pillaging hordes are monstrous losses for the West. And yet, there is a greatness in the rise, the essence, and the work of Genghis Khan and his loyal followers that must command the admiration of all who have an unspoiled sense for warrior greatness and soldierly dominion.

Here, for the first time, was an attempt to unleash the insurrection of martial barbarism, purely through willpower, against a cultivated but overly complacent world, vastly superior in every way. And that willpower triumphed!

Genghis Khan set the example that a fighting people must know no private life: he ordered total mobilization, encompassing every Mongol, man or woman, from child to elder. Those who did not bear arms had to work in labor services, administration, and the countless posts between homeland and front. Work, battle, honor, plunder, victory, and death were shared by all. Thus, it took a Genghis Khan to come into the world to teach Europe and its oppressive rulers of the potential for monumental deeds achievable by a totalized people!

But where were the blonde, invincible warriors of the North?

The year was twelve hundred after the birth of Jesus! The "peace of God," or rather the command of Yahweh, had descended upon the world and had struck the sword from the hand of the warlike North! The necks were bent, the hearts made peaceful, which is to say cowardly. The Germanic wildness, the magnificent berserker fury, the divine Nordic demonism had been diluted with baptismal water. Long had the heroic songs fallen silent, and instead, somber, joyless chorales, heavy as incense clouds, rose to the heavens. And wherever a lone pagan warrior, a heretic, dared to raise his head defiantly, the dark men lay in wait to murder him.

The conflict between emperor and pope cost streams of the finest German blood. And as the eyes of the Germans were fixed upon Rome, the source of all evil in Europe, the East faded from German sight, thus hindering any effective policy.

Countless thousands of the last longing warriors of the North joined the Crusader armies, seeking a proud end, at least, in a world that had become meaningless. They marched proudly and defiantly for an unworthy cause—a hollow grave that held no purpose, for the Christian was supposed to have ascended to heaven, not laid in a revered tomb, but seated at the right hand of God, beyond any pilgrimage, crusade, or warrior's journey!

Alexander III sat on the supposed throne of Peter in Rome—a hater of the North and of freedom, a fanatical dark man, a ruler of Yahweh's kingdom, and a scheming servant of the pale Christ—Alexander, who, under the motto of "divide and rule," delighted in igniting brotherly strife, in setting everyone against everyone! And Innocent III was a worthy successor to him!

Genghis Khan had to demonstrate to the world that entire continents—once flourishing, strong, and brave—must inevitably perish when clerics begin to rule in their way, and that lands thus weakened become easy prey for a few courageous souls.

Historiography readily condemns Genghis Khan for his bloody rule: not a single battle would the Mongols or any of his sons have initiated or won on Eastern European soil if the North had still been vigilant! But superstitious Christians babbled about a 'King David' and thought they should cheer him on—the Mongol, who had certainly not come to establish Yahweh's kingdom!

What, however, shakes all men who strive to fulfill the warrior's law is the fact that Genghis Khan had the iron law of the Mongols, the Raffa, inscribed on iron tablets. What was engraved there was nothing other than the internal law of the Mongol way—no foreign commandments, no distant rules, no promises, no heaven, and no hell.

The exact text of the Raffa is lost, but the fact that murder, theft, lies, and adultery vanished from the lives of the brave, and that loyalty, honor, courage, readiness to die, truthfulness, and belief in victory took root in their hearts, attests that this racial law was good. Better than the Gospels, which allowed a weary world to decay! And so powerful was this law, its understanding, and its effect, that even after Genghis Khan's death, the spirit of his race remained alive and continued to exert its influence. The structure of a world empire was held together by the racial law of the Rassa, the law that bound the loyal and the brave to duty and honor, so that their people's creator and leader remained among them, even though he had died.

Wherever courage, honor, and truthfulness shine as expressions of lawful conduct, the strong of the North feel reverence and respect. They understand that all racially pure peoples can rise to embrace such conduct, and thus they guard their minds against falling into racial chauvinism. However, pride in one's race is inseparable from the knowledge of the great potential power that arises from the harmony of blood and will.

Throughout all times, the Earth has been the place where values are tested, and thus the calling of the strong to justice—or it has become the playground for unrestrained, that is, duty-averse and honor-forgetting, greed. The strong of all peoples recognize each other as those who know the law. They will never see mutual extermination as their mission; instead, they will ensure that the rights to life—that is, the order and hierarchy suitable to the true values and authentic, brave nations—are justly respected. There are no hereditary feuds among strong, law-abiding peoples. Here, only struggles for the expansion of power may occur, though—when one right to life opposes another—this may go as far as eradication. Hereditary enmity exists only between the forces of light and those of darkness. In contrast, inherited hatred resides in the hearts of the inferior against the strong.

Every valuable race carries within its chest the consciousness of its mastery, and nothing is more natural than for the true master races to press toward the expression of the power that befits them, as a flower grows toward the light. That in this process of development, the inferior is pushed aside is only natural and therefore justified. The fault does not lie in the supposed brutality of the growing, but in the weakness and resistance-lessness of the perishing.

The brightest radiance, however, will come from the race that crowns the purest blood with the strongest will. This race may rightly boast of the divinity of its blood. The North is aware that its best were, in mythical ancient times, brothers of the Aesir! The pride of a master race is mightier than the religious feeling of being a member of a random, faith-driven community of the 'redeemed.'

Where the natural values of a nation have also outwardly asserted themselves through the recognition of the brave, there arises, through the deliberate eradication of all inferiority, an increasingly solid and ever-elevating visible core people. To keep this core people pure, to refine it further, and, if possible, to ennoble it in reproduction, is the ethical will of a people that rises above religions.

This ethos, directed at the eternity of this world, becomes the expression of the nation's heroic longing. It demands the highest commitment to the will to live, to grow higher, to overcome. It necessitates a masculine attitude of eternal striving for perfection, and thus leads to the eternal war of the just—those who stand in correct order—filling the Earth with creative restlessness, bold plans, revolutionary ideas, and brave deeds, freeing the world from the chaos of the idol of chance and returning it to the rhythm of the law.

The secret to outliving dying, sated peoples lies in the fact that the youthful peoples commit themselves to the ethos of their law-given duty and develop their power within this ethos. The North is endowed with all the prerequisites to survive the declines. The danger to its own decline lies only in its harmlessness, in its friendly inclination towards unmartial, forgiving kindness.

One essential task of the strong lies in keeping the North vigilant through their warrior spirit, stoking the fires of decay and renewal, and maintaining fear among the weak—what is the outcry of the weak worth in this? Will a living person really lie down to die alongside one who is perishing, just so the latter is not alone in death?

The strong do not demand that consideration be shown to them! Every consideration hinders forward movement, and only for the sake of this forward movement is life beautiful and worth living. The strong will also not argue with the weak over the meaning of life, for the weak can never grasp the profound meaning of the law that marks all weakness with the seed of death. Nor can anyone expect courage from the weak to confront the unveiled law that carries the death sentence.

The North has already wasted too much time in talking and negotiating, has missed too many moments through consideration, has left too many deeds undone through support of the weak. Therefore, in the moment of decision, it surveys the world one last time to hasten the resolve to act, guided by examples.

The examples that a person seeks and finds in history are the measure of the worth of their own longing. The pious may look toward the saints of renunciation and sacrifice to grant themselves permission to escape duty, but the strong seek and find the examples of strong life, which call their own lives to commitment, trial, and fulfillment. The examples of weakness, on the other hand, are for them the warning signs of the shallows and reefs on which the ship of life threatens to founder.

The heroic songs sung by the strong in their passion for life are filled with a hard rhythm. They sound like battle signals. They stir the blood and whip the nerves to make the final, decisive leap into the unknown.

The weak, on the other hand, know only the dull songs of weary sadness, sung in the dragging, monotonous, and soporific rhythm of chorales. Their laments are filled with the same despair as the Jewish psalms of lamentation, whose rhythm, tellingly, is like a limping gait. A great bridge spans the sorrows of the weak through all times, connecting the wretched into a vast horde that, like a plague of locusts, descends in torment, destruction, and desolation upon the fertile lands of the strong.

Against this march of the sorrowful, the strong stand firm, and their victory songs dispel the stifling dread that precedes the sorrowful like a dense fog, obscuring the sun, trees, and the distant horizon. The strong tear apart the veils of fear with their courage, allowing them to seek out danger like a hidden treasure. And every strong person hopes, at the end of their days, to find the company of warriors and heroes and to be deemed worthy of being welcomed by them as an equal.

Thus, the strong press through the mist of decay and the veil of fear, hoping to discover the gateway of action, behind which lies the homeland of the strong. And every hero whose example shines through the darkness of despair becomes a comrade to the strong.

One of the most glorious heroes, whose work inspires awe and reverence in the strong, is Theoderic, the great King of the Ostrogoths, whose deeds even a fifteen-hundred-year-old Christian veil could not obscure.

The mere fact that Theoderic was able to lead his people out of the chaos of the Huns and—saving them from a descent into a mongrelized mass—was able to march them in a firm formation through the turbulent Balkans and into Italy, proves the incredible boldness as well as the unique statesmanship of this man, whose word bound an entire people—not only warriors, but largely women, children, elders, burdened with livestock, provisions, and valuables—under a determined will.

This Gothic migration was more dangerous than a Viking voyage on fragile ships amidst stormy seas without a compass!

And what superiority of the race, what knowledge of the uniqueness of Germanic blood must have lived in this people, pledged solely to future freedom, to enable them to carve their way resolutely, mercilessly, and, if necessary, destructively; to resist the temptations of early satisfaction, wealth, and tranquility; and, above all, to preserve their blood from being tainted by foreign women and men!

Leader of the People!—such is the meaning of the name Theoderic.

A joyful proof of the triumph of a will rooted in belief in one's own strength is the successful march of the Goths, who, like the Æsir of northern antiquity, carved paths through hostile nations with swords in hand and, in the knowledge of future glory, endured the hardships of a present burdened by countless struggles and dangers without complaint.

How shameful it is, then, that Christians of German nationality admire the Bible stories of the Jews' wilderness wanderings, embellished with lies and boasting, and praise the mentality of this gang, which, moving in circles on a pathetically small territory, had to be comforted, pacified, or even fed by its Yahweh in times of danger!

The whole corruption of Mediterranean miracle beliefs is necessary to worship such a "divine story" as salvific and, alongside it, to forget the heroic history of a strong people who set out to build a kingdom in this world!

If anyone deserves for the young soldiers of the nation to make a pilgrimage to his grave for all eternity, to remember and pledge allegiance, it is Theoderic, whose dead body was indeed torn from his tomb in Ravenna and desecrated, but whose spirit has entered the eternal legacy of the Germanic peoples of this world.

How small are all the legends of mostly sickly, feeble saints beside the life stories of solitary heroes of Germanic blood! How small is the kingdom of the other world, measured against the fantasies of the saints, when compared to the mighty, bold, and defiant deeds that mark the birth of the kingdom of this world. How shabby are the haggling patriarchs and begging saints next to the proud, imperious warriors of the North!

And does not the paradise of the pious, with its harmless, knowledge-stifling fruits, appear like a life-removed, sultry hothouse compared to the blooming, fragrant, joyfully colored rose garden of the North, which loves beauty and therefore loves struggle?

Can Nordic blood even seriously debate what is more beautiful: desert sand or snow? Humility or rebellion? Grace or action? Prayer or sword?

Theoderic does not compete with saints for the favor of fickle masses; he calls upon the strong to witness his true, unveiled kingship.

Talents may be born, geniuses may grow, but heroes mature in decision, and superhumans only arise in times of great upheaval, when they stride over the ruins of decayed times, when they defy the waters of destruction like boulders, and dare the leap over the threshold of a new age.

Theoderic overcame the temptations that, in his youth, as with every growing person, also reached his heart. He overcame the dream and vanity, he overcame the splendor of wealth and, above all, the poison of luxury that was to be injected into his blood at the court of Byzantium, which had demanded and received him as a hostage. He learned that a man preparing for deeds must first become solitary and silent, that he must not squander his strength in frivolous moments. Thus, he was able to find his heart and, with it, his people.

And as he found his people, there awakened in him the will to lead this people to power, which means, to let it become a kingdom.

Indeed, the battles Theoderic had to fight were great, bloody, and cruel; indeed, they led him over hills of corpses and through seas of tears; indeed, his victories were radiant and unique. But all hardships and all victories were outshone by the radiant faith in the Germanic kingdom of this world, which poured an overwhelming longing into his heart, so that neither God nor Devil, neither Heaven nor Hell found room there.

Theoderic made himself entirely an instrument of his longing; he became a total man of the North.

Scarcely had he, after unimaginable hardships, succeeded in leading his people to Italy and, after years of wandering, bound them again to the soil, scarcely had he displaced and killed Odovacer, the former Germanic military leader who had elevated himself to regent, to Patricius of the western part of the Roman Empire alongside the shadow-emperor Romulus Augustulus, and thereby practically wiped out the Western Roman Empire, than he purposefully set to work to create space and kingdom not only for his people but for the entire Germanic race. A colossal plan! Germanic warriors were to be taken from the service of foreign conquerors, Germanic tribes, scattered and, in the long run, condemned to extinction, were to be united into a great, solid structure, into a kingdom, in order to find, instead of destruction through racial mixing, eternity through racial preservation!

But now, within Theoderic, the will for an empire arose! This uprising of the North had to represent an immense threat to the old, tired world! And indeed, the plan of the great Goth was perceived in this way!

Theoderic was careful to avoid coming into close contact with Rome. He allowed the Romans to remain as they were and had no intention of mixing their ways with Gothic, Germanic, or Nordic law. When he took control in Italy, he made Rome the city of administration but made Ravenna, Verona, and Bern his capitals.

What was Rome, after all? A city of pensioners, nothing more! A city whose citizens anxiously awaited the grain ships from Africa to receive their share of the tribute and then, as long as supplies lasted, to live carefree and without work on bread and games. Let Rome suffocate in its laziness; let it worship its shadow emperor. Theoderic kept his distance. He used the exemplary administration to prevent the vast country from falling into ruin with its complex tax system. He utilized the fearful and submissive officials to spare his state from disruptions. But he avoided Rome. Like the plague. For he was a heretic and wanted nothing to do with the Holy City and its poison-laden incense.

And Byzantium—Theoderic had come to know it too well in his youth to avoid, as much as possible, the certain treachery that lurked there. He had endured too many sad experiences to believe even a single word from Byzantium, let alone follow any of its advice.

Thus, Theoderic avoided above all becoming a pawn in the politics of foreign powers. He especially avoided, though it would have been easy, placing the imperial crown upon his head. Had he wished, Byzantium and Rome would have lain at his feet, begging for mercy. The entire world would have willingly opened its treasuries to the Goth, if only to save their bare lives. Theoderic took none of what was offered to him. He was thinking of the great Germanic Empire!

This is how the Germanic leader of the people differs from the un-Nordic imperialist!

The "enlightened" world—by which is meant one that has become feeble-kneed, soulless, and brittle—mockingly and pitifully accuses men and doers of Theoderic's caliber of fantasy and detachment from reality, not knowing that such a stance, as Theoderic displayed in his incorruptibility toward outward advantages, is the highest form of wisdom! Imperialists, sooner or later, die either by the sword or from stomach ulcers! And the people they lead, in every sense of the word, suffer the same fate. Only where the frenzy of greedy imperialism is replaced by the national ideal of a world-bound, eternal empire does an awakened and, yes, dangerous life arise!

Out of this knowledge, Theoderic was able to laugh and set aside all thoughts of the imperial crown, the purple, Rome, and Byzantium. He knew that if the empire became his, eternity, too, would be his. And in this eternity, he understood, are also contained all the external values of this world.

Theoderic was not understood by many of his contemporaries. They were neither the wisest nor the most honest, nor the bravest who opposed him, internally or sometimes even outwardly. They were mostly the envious, the careerists, the unoriginal, or even the bribed. They were the spiritual descendants of those miserable half-hearted men who, four centuries earlier, had struck from Arminius, the liberator, the weapon of revolt, thereby robbing him of the preconditions for an empire.

Theoderic was the man capable, with his superior will and equally superior tenacity, of waiting for the death of his opponents—or even hastening it when necessary.

The power of his vision of an empire was mightier than the fury of the envious. At times, his loyal followers found it difficult to accompany him on the intellectual path of spiritually starving his opponents. They were far more inclined to strike and create the empire with fire and sword. But Theoderic thought of the substance of the nation, of the precious blood of the race. And for the future of the Germanic national power, he avoided all unnecessary bloodshed.

Slowly, perhaps at times even too slowly, he approached his goal. But the strength of the people grew, and where otherwise burial mounds would have risen over the dead bodies of brave northern warriors, the blooming children of men whom death had passed by because Theoderic loved life, were at play! Thus, toward the end of his life, which was filled with an unprecedented struggle, Theoderic had only two serious opponents left: Clovis of the Franks and the Pope in Rome!

These two opponents, however, threw themselves with all their might into the breach to prevent the formation of the empire. The breaches consisted of the particularist ambitions of the Frankish kingdom, which under Clovis sought power, clashing with Theoderic's will, and the imperialistic papacy, which feared the northern uprising and suspected Arianism as a Germanic rebellion.

Anyone who knows even remotely the cold, calculating power politics of the Cross and its representative in Rome, the Pope, who would not hesitate to ally even with the so-called Devil, will find it self-evident that the Pope immediately used the dagger in the person of Clovis to eliminate Theoderic before he could reach his imperial goal. Equally self-evident is the fearful haste of those who felt threatened, trying as quickly as possible to erase all traces of the crime in a world conflagration. The Pope and the Frank incited unrest in the world to make the birth of the empire at least difficult, if not to strangle the young empire in its moment of birth. In this rage, Pope and Frank have always been alike. Theoderic felt this, as later did Bismarck, when Rome instigated the Kulturkampf to destroy the newly achieved unity of the Second Empire!

The Pope hated Theoderic as only a Christian can hate a heretic who does not submit to the dogma and therefore to the power of the Church.

Nothing compares to the destructive hatred of the Cross, which condemns to death all that stands against the ultimate dominion of Yahweh through a natural will to life. The Cross jealously ensures that the prerequisites for Judgment Day—that is, the cessation of all independent life—are fulfilled. Every fanatical Christian who sees himself as a conscious, will-executing member of the "Christian race" pursues a systematic policy of annihilation against every true race. Thus, the head of the knowing "Christian race," the Pope in Rome, repeatedly leads his legions onto the world's battlefield to secure the empire for Yahweh.

In his vision of the empire, Theoderic initially, and perhaps unconsciously, challenged the highest goal the Cross had to defend—the total empire of Yahweh, encompassing heaven and earth.

It is certain that Theoderic did so initially without full awareness; he was a heretic, an Arian. But when he saw that the threads of Christian politics led to the courts of his adversaries, particularly to Clovis, he became a conscious mortal enemy of the papacy and thus of Christian imperialism.

Was Theoderic a Christian? Yes, he was baptized! But his Christianity was shaped by Arianism. It was not oriented toward the otherworldly; it cared nothing for the one who was to come to judge the living and the dead, to establish the kingdom of Yahweh! Arianism rejected the myth of Christ's divine sonship and thereby the very soul of Christianity. Arianism thought in a Germanic way—that is, it was ethically oriented. It was folk-centered! Thus, it resisted the imperialistic claims of the Cross; thus, it opposed the Pope!

For centuries, from council to council, imperialistic Christianity pursued Arianism to eradicate the ethnic thought from the world and with it the last vestige of freedom. Is it any wonder that persecuted freedom found refuge with the Germans? Is it any wonder, too, that the Cross found yet another reason to eradicate even the last German who still carried the seed of future heresy in his blood!

Theoderic knew that his empire had to be free of Rome; therefore, he accepted no Catholics into his inner circle, and for a Goth under Theoderic, it was impossible to become Catholic. From the North Sea, from the amber coast of the East, down to Africa, the Rome- and thus Cross-free empire of the Germanic race and Nordic blood was to extend. An extraordinarily bold plan, which in its ultimate consequence meant nothing less than expelling the Cross from Europe and ultimately driving it over Byzantium back to Jerusalem.

Under Theoderic, the North made its first counterstrike against the Jahwist desert mindset!

The worldly empire prepared to storm the heavens of Sinai. Prometheus and Lucifer, Odin and Baldur clashed against Yahweh, Moses, the prophets, the Messiah, and his emissaries! A splendid image of rebellion, a blazing signal of attack that the warlike North launched in the last hour of the old pagan humanity, which was simultaneously the first hour of a grand Germanic Empire in this world. The Pope paled, the Cross wavered, and Yahweh hid his face in the clouds of Sinai.

Then the Pope found his way to the Frank!

Messengers rode from him to the North. Messengers returned to Rome. Clovis became Catholic! Like a blind but malevolent Höðr, he took up the fatal mistletoe in his right hand and prepared to throw. Though Theoderic could evade the blow, the Frankish kingdom remained a living, poisonous reality, a breach and a stake in Theoderic's Germanic Empire!

The very fact that Clovis crawled to the Cross for "political" reasons illuminates the peculiar circumstances of his baptism! He, the deceived deceiver, became a servant of the Pope. His Frankish kingdom became the poisoned arrow of Yahweh's total empire against the Germanic empire in this world.

Take note: Clovis moved from paganism to Catholicism! His hatred for the Arian Theoderic and his vision of empire distorted his view of real political circumstances! While Theoderic rooted his people in new soil, gave them land and a firmly structured home, and sought to grant them eternity through the empire, Clovis and his bought followers undermined the foundation of the future from within, from the soul!

For a short time, Theoderic managed to halt Clovis's intrigues. And in that time, he prepared to deliver a fatal blow against the Pope and his imperialism. The great king planned to strangle Rome by surprise, strip the Cross of its power, destroy the Church, and eliminate the Pope. In the pure air, the citizens of the Germanic Empire were to breathe, with no clouds of incense to befog the minds of men or cloud their gaze into the boundless future.

Already, the Pope had been thrown into prison; the decrees were prepared to close Catholic churches, chapels, prayer houses, and monasteries. The Pope died, and Yahweh's emissaries trembled at the certain end!

The warriors for Theoderic's empire, the land of the free, the homeland of the strong in this world, crouched, ready for the final leap. The sword for the first liberating blow already shone in their hands: then Theoderic had to die.

He had to die!

His death was agonizing, unexpected. The men who witnessed the torturous death of the great Goth wept uncontrollably. Everyone knew: Theoderic had to die at the appointed time.

Poison!

It was said then, and it is still known today!

Theoderic died, and the empire of the Germans did not become reality. It died, as the Cross wished, in the hour of its birth. The Germanic tribes and nations, according to the will of the vengeful "God," remained largely alone in the swiftly reimposed scattering.

Pope Gregory, whom Christians, as particularly ruthless imperialists, call "the Great," tells of a hermit who fled from the world and its masculine struggles, claiming to have seen with his own eyes that two angels of Yahweh carried Theoderic's dead body through the air up to the highest heavens. From there, they threw him down into the deepest depths of hell, into the crater of Stromboli!

Thus, Theoderic was punished by the Cross as a second Lucifer, thus he was cursed and damned by Yahweh for all eternity as a rebel, the rebel of the North!

The bells of Rome rang out in triumph, and the heretics perished on the pyres. And the empire of Yahweh seemed invincible.

Theoderic the Great, who had once set out to create a homeland for the strong, found no place in either this world or the next. Thus, he had to enter the eternal wandering of the cloud-like idea and become myth. As Dietrich of Bern, he became the embodiment of all German longing. And it is Dietrich whom people imagine as Emperor Barbarossa, slumbering in the mountain, waiting for the resurrection of the Empire. All myths, beginning with Wodan, the wild hunter, and leading to the Christmas Man, who may pass through the invisible Germanic realm of the North only on the holiest of holy nights, at the hour of the Nordic birth of light and hope, to encourage the strong, reward the good, and frighten the wicked, are crowned in the myth of Theoderic and his first Germanic Empire in this world.

An empire that will come as a homeland for the strong!

About three centuries after Clovis's soulless act of betrayal, the rival empire of the Franks was led to victory over the dream of Theoderic that had become an ideal: Charles, who is also fondly called "the Great," arose and "united" part of the northern lands in his imperialistic manner.

In comparison to Theoderic, Charles is of no remarkable greatness, to say nothing of comparing the two imperial ideals! It is high time we stopped associating the first Germanic empire with Charles. Theoderic is our forefather, not Charles!

And every time men rose to fight for the freedom and greatness of the empire, they were the descendants of the folk spirit of Theoderic. The imperialistic spirit of Charles of the Franks was and remained foreign and repugnant to them. To say nothing of Widukind—yet whose heirs were they all, Heinrich I, Otto I, Konrad II? They dreamed the dream of the Northern Empire and swore allegiance to the spirit of Dietrich of Bern! They had to atone for the fact that a Clovis had once crawled to the Cross. The spiritual successors of the Frank are those pitiable "Cross figures" who, under the names of Louis the Pious and Otto III, no longer knew that once men had yearned for a North free from Rome!

All emperors and kings who inherited Theoderic's legacy of longing had to experience what it meant not to have an Arian, heretical, and thus this-worldly, loyal people behind them, but rather a mass, the majority of whom were manipulated by Roman priests.

For the honor of the great German, let it be stated once more that Theoderic intended to build the nation from the values of blood, soul, and race. Thus, Theoderic thought and acted in a folk-centered way. Charles, however, stood as a stranger to this way of thinking: he was an imperialist! Theoderic could never have become Catholic. Charles, on the other hand, would never have had a feeling for ethics, for Arianism, for heresy! For Theoderic, the soul was the matter of the people; for Charles, religion was a matter of the state!

Here, the spirits finally parted ways.

Later emperors and kings fought desperate battles to wrest their greatly diminished empire from the grip of papal imperialism, and since they could not divert their eyes for even a moment from the danger posed by the Cross, the empire's structure, held together only with great effort, continued to fall apart.

The links of the chain—the tribes and states—lacked inner strength, as their peoples had to surrender their soul to Rome. Thus, the links had to break, to crumble. The East became prey to the Slavs, the West a pawn of Rome, becoming an adversary of the empire, while the South collapsed entirely.

Yet the more this world and its structure crumbled, the higher the Cross rose, and its shadow eventually filled the entire world, so much so that the sun lost its light.

But in the night, the last of the surviving strong ones, the longing, the young, climbed the mountains of freedom to ignite the torches of their faith and to send their defiant songs into the night of hatred as a declaration of a steadfast faith in the coming empire of this world.

And when freedom seemed to have vanished from this world, a star shone from the night sky, guiding the seekers out of chaos and turmoil: Dietrich, the most loyal of the loyal, the true guardian of the drink of remembrance.

No act undertaken for freedom and for the humanity bound to it is ever in vain, even if it fails. As long as the will is fervent, incorruptible, and genuine, the deed lives on forever! This has been the steadfast hope of all rebels who, without thanks or reward, without the prospect of ultimate victory, took on the risk of action solely for the sake of honor and duty.

The will to freedom is immortal, even if it rests as an almost extinguished spark beneath the ashes of failure. A gust of wind can blow away the ashes and rekindle the spark into a bright flame, a flame capable of reducing mighty structures to rubble.

From the North came the fire into the world, and with the fire came the understanding of the will's eternity, for it is the will that created the fire. In the North, too, resides the demonic urge to be a bearer of fire.

In a later time, the demonic force of fire-bearing was diluted into crude, chauvinistic schoolmastery. That was when the empire was no longer an ideal but merely a matter of administration! That was when people forgot Theoderic and placed the pale Messiah above Dietrich!

The radiant dignity of a leader of Germanic blood and Nordic spirit has always been the distinctive mark of his power. The nobility of these royal people was demonstrated in a superior attitude, unyielding pride, a readiness for solitude, and disdain for all those outward trappings that are supposed to make the life of an ordinary person "valuable."

The unmatched greatness of the North lies not only in having produced individual royal figures but in having birthed an entire race of such royal people.

A single tribe of this race would have sufficed to provide rulers to all the states of the earth! And it is more than a myth that again and again, in the legends and tales of distant peoples, a white god appears, coming from the North, to lead nations toward the glory of a courageous life. Notably, this is a white god for an entire people! And the fact that not only primitive African tribes but also ancient races like the Chinese and the Incas reverently erected monuments to the white god in expectation demonstrates the immense superiority of Nordic spirit and the Germanic connection to light.

Wherever in the world the Northman set foot on foreign soil, people bent before his humanity, before this radiant dignity. Even the Romans had to admit that their own humanity faltered in comparison to that of the North.

A race of kings!

This also entails, however, the danger of dispersal. Slave races can easily be held together and compelled toward so-called happiness by a superior despot. But it is difficult for a superior man to claim authority over others who are also superior. Therefore, it is anything but a sign of barbarity and lack of culture when the royal race of the North resisted being ruled. It is only through the lens of the kingship of this race that we can understand why it limited itself to recognizing, in times of war, the bravest of the brave as the champion and granting him the right to command in battle.

The entire inner tragedy of the North lies in the fact that it gave birth only to kings, not to servants, reckoning only with the light, never with the shadow of this world. Among kings, trust and faithfulness are the sole forms of law; among slaves and merchants, however, cunning rules.

Foreign despots can issue commands to a people that kneel in silent reverence before the throne, blindly obeying a single will, the will of the despot, without question or judgment. Such a people can endure anything—even injustice, caprice, and cruelty from the despot—and even believe these are attributes of true power. They fear these traits, though they would not want to be without them.

Foreign races struggled to connect with their distant gods. The chasms were so vast and yawning that they needed a mediating caste, the priests, to receive revelations of divine will. In the "people of God" of the Jews, the highest priest was clothed with the insignia of power and given dominion. The Jews initially viewed it as a decline when, over time, a kingship developed alongside the priestly caste. However, they allowed the priest to anoint the king, thus directly connecting him to divinity. But the fact that the anointed king was inevitably of lesser power than the one who anointed him, namely the priest, was so self-evident that it did not need to be stated. Without the oil of anointing, there was no crown! This outlook shaped the political thought of Christianity, which sought to cast its shadow over the world.

The royal race of the North knew no oil of anointing. Theoderic was a ruler through his superior humanity. Only with Charles was the anointing oil of Rome poured upon a king's head—the oil of Rome that directed Yahweh's will into the world! This is more than a mere outward sign. With Charles, a despot was set over the royal race. As a result, the royal people of the North had to become rebels, defenders of true kingship against a despotism that no longer demanded loyalty but submission to the divine will of the anointed one.

Is it any wonder that from the time of Charles onward, rebels often thought and acted more royally than the anointed kings? True kingship lived in the brave hearts of the strong, against whom the "holy war" was declared. The revolutions of the so-called democratic rabble raged against the kingship of the heart, which saved men from humility but not from the stake and the guillotine. And that the leaders of the rabble revolts were ultimately guardians of the anointing oil is anything but inexplicable!

In the democracies that the Cross established in its battle against the royal race, the idea of the "Christ King" emerges more and more clearly as a calculated attempt at Asiatic despotism.

"The Lord alone is King, I am but a withered flower!"

Woe to the royal woman, the future bearer of royal children!

The stake is near, and a reason to condemn her to a fiery death is quickly found.

Woe to the royal woman, the sorceress!

Woe to the warrior, the uncrowned king

Who moves across the world from the North!

Woe to the warrior, for he will fall prey to the Christ King,

Who wrenches the sword from his weary hand to break it.

Woe to the warrior who accepts the welcome drink from the foreign king. The drink is poisoned!

"The Lord will be King forever and ever!"

Woe to the royal race, for it must die for the sake of the kingdom of the One, Yahweh!

"Yahweh is King over all the earth."

"He makes the counsel of the nations futile and thwarts the thoughts of the peoples."

"Come and behold the works of Yahweh, who is so wondrous in his deeds among the children of men."

"They shall have one single king over them."

Thus began the hunt against the royal race, against the proud humanity of the North.

Tens of thousands fell, struck down by poisoned arrows.

The blood of entire proud, unbowed lineages spilled into the sand, before it could bear heirs and avengers in their children.

The race of the North became homeless!

———————————

But today, as the strong rise to create a homeland for their race in this world for all eternity, the awakening of racial awareness makes the despots of the Cross tremble.

The doctrine of race once again finds law and its certainty. And there, where this law, like the victorious sun, pierces through clouds and twilight, the last wisps of fog are dispelled.

Day is dawning!

And this day is the beginning of new rule and glory for the royal race, whose strongest have kept the chalice of life's essence from spilling.

Now tremble, Yahweh, for your kingdom!

———————————

The boldest warriors of the North, the true guardians of the Grail of the Germanic Empire, were at the same time the fiercest enemies of Yahweh and his kingdom.

Freedom of the soul for the ultimate bond to the empire of this world! This was the hidden pole of their longing.

Many of the rebels and insurgents could not shape this idea of freedom into clear words; for many, the longing could only express itself in the confused stammering of a troubled heart. Yet all of them felt instinctively drawn to actions that would sever the ties to Yahweh's kingdom.

Tragic is the misunderstanding of the causes of bondage, a misunderstanding shown by the fact that some rebels cried out for a new god, attributing his existence to some ambiguous chapter of the Bible. The king Yahweh was then quick to appear in a new, more modern guise.

But the clearer the understanding of the strong grew, the more the longing of the solitary ones rose to the realm of the ideal, from which hidden connections became apparent, and the greater and more relentless became their resolve to create a homeland.

This idea of homeland was directed less toward the present than toward the future. The present proved to be rotten, cowardly, and malicious. That the solitary ones could nevertheless believe in the seed of eternal life even in a diseased present demonstrates the selflessness of their actions and the true daemonic nature of their perseverance, which rose above any form of self-centered thought.

Every believer in the future who committed honor and life to the coming empire of this world must inevitably become a rebel against the kingdom of that other world. In the eyes of Yahweh, the great heroes of this world were, without exception, "blasphemers." The more they loved their nation, the more dangerous they became to "heaven," and the more superior their stance against its emissaries became.

The rebels of the North, looking down from the heights of their ideals into the depths of superstitious daily life, began their song of victory. Through their superior knowledge, they became mockers, despisers, even "blasphemers" of all that might be sacred to fools. Anyone among the great of this world who gained insight into the troubles of the everyday and the schemes of the otherworldly felt defiantly superior and could smile knowingly, even on the pyre. What could the threats of madmen mean to a free man's soul? The much-celebrated pagan laughter is nothing but the confident smile of the knowing, whose joy springs from the certainty of a strong heart.

Some of the hardest revolutionaries and the most subversive thinkers were often also the most joyful and open-hearted people when, in the company of like-minded souls, they could bare their hearts.

One of the most joyful and at the same time dangerous among the rebels of the spirit, among the Vikings of the soul who set out for the land of the strong, was Ulrich von Hütten. His humanity is all the more captivating and inspiring for those conscious of their blood who enter the realm of his ideas and the scope of his plans. And from Nietzsche, the dynamite of the North, comes the concept of "The Joyful Science."

The colder the air, the brighter the glaciers can shine! Men of the seas are capable of sharper vision than those who live in the confinement of dull valleys!

A bold, joyful pagan laughter resonates from the "Letters of the Obscure Men" that Hütten wrote together with his companion Rubianus. One can still feel today how these two young fellows held their sides with laughter as they let their quills dance across the pages, mocking the "dark men," caricaturing their puffed-up strutting, infecting an entire world with their laughter! The entire vitality of the young, the unspent, the life-believing is in this deadly laughter, in this acid-sharp mockery, in this taunting that only the sick and the affected accuse of being "heartless." The afflicted immediately put on a sour-sweet face and asked that the battle be conducted "objectively"! Nothing is as deadly as the mockery of the superior; that is why the weak at all times claim that mockery is "nihilistic" and demand discussion instead! As if a straight-grown man could enter into a discussion with a hunchback about the possible virtues of a hump! And does the hunchback think he could talk the healthy man into accepting a hump? The mentally hunchbacked will always try to portray their suffering as a blessing and to shine with the vanity known to the sick. Hütten laughed at them. And the more outraged they became, the heartier his laughter grew!

He knew that only heroes should be granted the honor of a duel, while for cowards, whose poisoned weapon is the tongue, the flat side of the sword suffices as punishment!

Hütten is a particularly instructive example of the inner development of a revolutionary, whose initial rebellion stems from blood and instinct, gradually and unstoppably ascending to the clear and cold zone of conscious and total revolutionary thought, with the goal of freedom and glory for the nation as the collective will, as the homeland of the strong.

Growth is the manifestation of life striving toward fulfillment. Revolution is the violent removal of forces hostile to growth, the shattering of life-destroying encrustations by the life seed, the emergence of the unspoiled primal layer awaiting the new seed, fulfillment, and fruition.

The revolutions of the spirit are vastly intensified revelations of the law that shatters the encrustations of cowardice, falsehood, and arbitrariness. The bearers of these revolutions are men who make themselves instruments of the law, executors of the will to life. The law often takes such exclusive possession of these vessel-making men that they must appear as demons to their surroundings. The world trembles when the revolutionaries of the law, carrying the explosive of truth in their souls, launch their assault to break down the gates that would block entry to a new millennium.

As with every true revolutionary, it is impossible to pinpoint historically when Hütten "became" a rebel. Rather, the rebellious spirit ferments beneath the surface until a strong impulse brings about its breakthrough. The revolutionary development follows a natural law. After an initial chaotic, fiery upheaval, it becomes over time clearer, colder, more conscious, and more effective. Revolutionary sentiment cannot be instilled but can certainly be awakened. This awakening occurs through experience, example, or insight. In Hütten's case, both experience and insight played an equal role in awakening his revolutionary spirit.

Hütten was born with stormy blood and a knightly disposition. Added to this was the daemonic spirit of a will for freedom and a fanatical love of truth.

The experience of oppression matured Hütten's longing for freedom, and this longing, in turn, sought the understanding of a purpose, the answer to the question of life's "why."

Like many thoughtless, "well-meaning" parents, Hütten's parents dedicated their firstborn to the Church. This superstitious custom has its roots in ancient

Judaism, which sought to "appease" Yahweh with the offering of a firstborn, including the first child, to make Him gracious and generous. The child, as a sacrifice, was given no consideration; as an object, it was completely excluded, and since, according to belief, it was "safe in Yahweh's hands," the parents need not concern themselves with the sacrifice of the firstborn but could even boast of having performed a good deed for the spiritual benefit of the one sacrificed.

In the monastery school at Fulda, to which the sacrifice had been taken, the young Hütten experienced the cruel compulsion of spiritual and mental discipline. Thousands of young people had previously gone through the same spiritual terror without resisting, without becoming rebels, perhaps even without becoming fully aware of the compulsion. In Hütten, however, the oppression hardened his resistance, encouraging independent thought and thus counter-pressure. Fortunately for the young rebel, the freedom-loving, independent Crotus Rubianus was often in Fulda. Through time spent with this skeptical mocker, the spark of longing in Hütten's soul was repeatedly rekindled into a bright flame until one day the time for escape had come. This escape, as is almost always the case, was intended as an excursion into the open "world." The romantic ecstasy that usually accompanies such an excursion and the first few miles quickly dissipates, giving way to a profound disillusionment. Each fugitive must first experience that the "world" is not at all hospitable, but rather quite resistant, that it awaits being won and shaped! This realization shatters the romantic fugitive, who falls away in bitterness and disgust—or strengthens in ever-greater defiance until he grows into the realm of the ideal, which—as the soul's mainland—can no longer be shaken.

Schiller experienced this no differently than Frederick the Great, and Heinrich von Kleist, through his fate, became a myth reflected in Nietzsche's Zarathustra.

All fugitives rushing into the land of their expectations to find freedom experience the same disillusionments, whether this land is America, with its promise of boundless possibilities, or Prussia, with the honor of a Freiherr vom Stein! There is no paradise of freedom; there are only lands where the conditions for freedom have been established. But freedom itself must be won and lived; it is not freely given, and even less can it be bought.

The young Hütten initially sought the promised land of freedom in the realm of knowledge, of education. It almost goes without saying that he did not find this land as an island or as a solid mainland. The universities were strongholds of intellectual obscurantism, and the cities were filled with smug arrogance or profit-driven hostility toward the spirit. The courts, as much as the castles, were preoccupied with concerns and struggles for personal power and the accompanying need to consider the politics of the day and its limited possibilities.

Hütten endured the trial of this realization; indeed, he grew through the understanding that oppression always spreads the same atmosphere, whether it takes root in monasteries, universities, or at courts! The fact that this realization was not paid for with death—either through suicide or the downfall of a disillusioned soul—is the first evidence Hütten provided of his right to be considered a revolutionary. In literary terms, this means that Hütten's life did not tragically end with the chapter of Suffering, but rather continued with a first sequel, the chapter of Overcoming, and went on to write the third chapter, Proving.

Since Hütten did not find freedom as a solid land or as an already-won form, he did the only thing a life-believing conqueror can do: he went out to seek people of his own spirit with whom he could find community, hoping that this community of mind and soul would become a community of life itself.

Through his search, his overcoming, and his struggle, Hütten teaches that a revolutionary passes through three realms, so to speak. The first realm is the realm of his dream, for the sake of which he sets out. The second realm is the attempt to establish new roots after setting out. The third realm, however, grows out of the realization that only by creating a new humanity can true homeland be made. While the second realm is an attempt to live under the compromise of disillusionment, only the third realm is fulfillment!

Hütten tore up his "citizenship" of the second realm on the road between Gotha and Erfurt. Here he realized that it was impossible and unworthy to live in a self-chosen circle of like-minded people as if it were a new homeland. The few free-spirited people who, like him, had gathered around the venerable Mutian to live day by day in the enthusiasm for beauty and truth, without having duty or attachment to the national community guide their lives, suddenly appeared to him like cowardly gamblers, playing with the cheap stake of their existence for the highest stake, the fulfillment of life.

From this experience, Hütten gained the insight that true life demands proving oneself, which means creating a nation that springs from the hearts of the strong. He realized that a fellowship of enthusiasts was nothing more than a caricature of the true, the third realm. This insight turned him into a politician who entered the struggle to transform the despicable present so that it could lay the groundwork for the future of the true realm.

His polemics against obscurantism and for the freedom of knowledge gave way more and more to writings addressed to the nation. Hütten realized that a new, liberated nation would also bring about a new, free science, and not the other way around; the liberation of science would not herald a new age for the nation.

Hütten is the first herald of the revolutionary knowledge of our time, that all great historical deeds are always directed toward the freedom and honor of a community, a people, a nation, as their ultimate goal.

What the non-revolutionary, content-with-the-times, status-accepting, "bourgeois" person would condemn as instability—this relentless drive forward, overcoming yesterday and today, the unconditional change of position—is one of the proofs of the authenticity of Hütten's creative freedom ideal. He willingly took on the accumulation of suffering and disappointment associated with frequent changes of position for the sake of the ideal and joyfully exchanged the certain hardship of an uncertain future for any unworthy security of familiarity.

The growth of opposition is the first sign of the danger posed by a determined innovator. The more detours the innovator seeks to avoid resistance and setbacks, the more strength he must waste on trivialities that only lead to the fragmentation of the force and impact of his assault. Moreover, prolonged compromise can lead to a dangerous weakening of one's character. Bismarck's saying that politics corrupts character is the cry of a straightforward man who despairs at the corruption of the current state and is consciously fearful of the ultimate ruthlessness of his own will.

It may be that the compromiser achieves greater immediate successes; indeed, it sometimes seems that only through compromise can ideas be transformed into action. However, actions that shake and shape an entire era are always carried out by relentless, uncompromising leaders. It matters little whether the revolutionary reaps the fruits of his actions or whether he must pass the sword of his spirit into the hands of his comrades before the decisive blow. The clearer Hütten's insight and the stronger his will for fulfillment became, the fewer friends he had. His companions of the second realm first withdrew in horror: the transition from a fundamentally harmless idea to a reality fraught with danger appeared to them not only questionable but profoundly undesirable. Men like the highly learned Erasmus, who longed for intellectual freedom, and Reuchlin, highly educated yet submissive to dark spiritual forces, had built temples of knowledge and fortresses of thought, but the land that was the homeland of their longing could only be reached through hidden doors to which only the initiated held the key of learning.

When Hütten broke out from the purely intellectual realm of the educated of his time, he was condescendingly pitied as a "barbarian." However, pity was soon followed by dismay and terror at the daemonic force of his forward drive.

To the end of his days, Hütten remained grateful for the education of humanism, to which he had contributed significant traits in its German form. But education was not an end in itself for him; it served as a weapon against ignorance. Ultimately, Hütten owed it to his humanistic education that he could fully grasp the revolutionary implications of Laurentius Valla's work exposing the papal deceit and the Christian forgery known as the "Donation of Constantine." The realization of these unscrupulous forgeries and the Christian strategy of suppressing and destroying the spirit that valued freedom gave Hütten clarity that the worldview rooted in the Church expressed itself in a ruthless politics of power.

In the political struggle that now began, Hütten had to prove—and could prove—that his realm meant a conscious growth beyond the half-measures-satisfied world of the humanists. The papacy, the crowning institution of political Christianity, viewed this realm with suspicion and attempted to keep its citizens on puppet strings. Hütten's realm, however, with its nation-centered thinking, encountered fierce opposition from the Pope.

When Hütten looked for allies, he found himself standing alone on the front lines. Erasmus bowed toward Rome and pledged the loyalty of his purely intellectual intentions. Reuchlin buried himself in his Kabbalistic studies and was relieved and grateful if he could enjoy the peace necessary for them. Rubianus was content with his promising career prospects. None of the citizens of humanism dared the leap into the ultimate great adventure; none wished to steer their life's ship over the dark, tumultuous sea of risk toward a new homeland.

Emperor Maximilian had once crowned the young poet Hütten in Augsburg, but he regarded the radical politician Hütten with skepticism, if not outright fear. Maximilian, like most princes of his time, was a friend of peaceful reconciliation and, wherever feasible, a proponent of peaceful world conquest through marriages and inheritances; he must have found Hütten's war cry disruptive! Hütten's war cry is to be understood literally! His goal was to arm Germany, supposedly to preempt the looming Turkish threat. In reality, Hütten did not consider the Turks particularly dangerous; what seemed dangerous to him was only Germany's fundamental defenselessness, as well as the indecision, jealousy, and spiritual instability of the ruling princes and their houses.

Only the awakening of a warrior instinct and the revival of military virtues could be thrown into the balance against this. Note: Hütten was the first to see the mobilization of the nation as the prerequisite for a spiritual revolution emanating from the warriors, and the resulting total national unity of the Germans!

An extraordinarily bold and unique idea, one that even a valiant knight and royal soldier like Sickingen could not comprehend. Sickingen was a rebel by his station, a fighter against the class of princes, clergy, and burghers that suppressed the free and manly knighthood, but at heart, he was a man fighting for a reservation. For the sake of this reservation, Sickingen even engaged in negotiations with Francis of France without hesitation. It was likely fortunate for the isolated Hütten that Sickingen only instinctively sensed in him the subverter of the knightly reservation, or Hütten's end would have been even more solitary and shameful!

Sickingen could never have understood the deep necessity of the peasants' uprising, much less their inclusion in the future German nation. Hütten had to acknowledge this with a sigh when, out of loyalty to his friend, he supported Sickingen's hopeless knightly revolt at Trier, which was undertaken at the most unfavorable time, thereby knowingly consigning himself to ruin.

Where even a Sickingen closed his eyes in horror before an abyss he found intolerable, a citizen of the second realm of the soul, Luther, completely despaired. Luther was a peasant rebel with all the positive but also all the clumsy qualities that entailed—a Michael Kohlhaas-like nature in the realm of conscience and soul. He sought to grasp the hand of God to anchor himself on the firm ground of faith's certainty and peace in God's refuge, even as Hütten had long since rejected this supposed saving hand to seek the worldly realm, the German nation of the strong.

Despite numerous forays that often brought him to the gates of the worldly realm, Luther repeatedly returned to theocentric thinking, to the pole of salvation through grace. Initially, he believed as much in the possibility of reforming the Christian Catholic Church as he later believed—in his second, far more valuable stage of development—in the possibility of doing without a visible Church, without a priesthood. Finally, he believed in the possibility of an evangelical sub-church reliant on divinely appointed authority, overshadowed by secular rule. Hütten, with his nation-centered, church-weary, messiah-rejecting vision of fulfillment, was unbearable to him, while Hütten, on the other hand, recognized and respected Luther as a transition from a theocentric to a nation-centered view of life. He felt a bond with Luther above all in their shared hatred of Rome, the source of all poison. Hütten repeatedly sought common ground and alliance with the second Luther. However, the third Luther created an unbridgeable divide between himself and Hütten. The gravedigger, however, was Melanchthon.

Melanchthon, already physically ill-favored, significantly influenced the transition of the second Luther to the third, leading Luther's spiritual trajectory to veer sharply upward after a brief approach to the Germanic realm of this world, only to end up in the realm of the other world. Melanchthon is the father of the Augsburg Confession, that deceptive bridge that leads trusting souls away from the realm of this world into the cloud-land of a new world, which is nothing but a reflection of the old, defeated Jahwist afterlife!

The peasant rebel Luther, who, in honest anger, nailed his theses against the spiritual cow-trade of indulgences—essentially a business transaction between the Pope, the Emperor, the princes, and the banking consortium of the Fuggers— to the door of the Castle Church in Wittenberg, thereby unknowingly and unintentionally striking at the most sensitive political sore, became increasingly overshadowed by theology. In the end, he, who initially only wanted to serve his fellow Germans and earnestly strove to bring justice and order to the German nation for the sake of heaven, ultimately surrendered his free will entirely and submitted himself to the arbitrary, predestining grace of the Lord Zebaoth, the King Yahweh, leaving man only humble submission.

The profound influence once exerted on him by the mystical text Theologia Deutsch, which had nearly brought him to the point of breaking away from Church-bound Christianity, faded as he returned to lifeless theological thought and reasserted that humanity, its peoples, and nations were ultimately nothing more than objects of blessing or curse in God's salvation plan. Where could the points of contact between the third Hütten and the third Luther possibly be?

For such an approach, Hütten would have had to use the "heavenly ladder" of the afterlife believers, which he found so ridiculous, or Luther would have had to abandon the grace-filled hand of God, which he deemed so essential! Since Luther also believed that the evil condition and unfortunate present were part of God's salvation plan, he lacked the ideological foundation to be a revolutionary. The means of rebellion was, in his view, condemnable, given his commitment to a life of prayer. For Luther, the secret of success in this world rested solely in the "merciful God." Therefore, to him, glorifying action beyond prayer had no value and could only be presumptuous.

"With our own strength, nothing is achieved; we are lost almost immediately!"

This statement for Luther is a clear affirmation of the immutable decree of the heavenly King from eternity.

My good works, they counted for nothing;
they were all tainted.
Free will hates God's judgment; it was dead to goodness.

This is the renunciation of the fundamental stance of Germanic morality—defiant resistance—in favor of humble submission. It is an unparalleled tragedy, one of the greatest tragedies of the North, that a man like Luther, honestly determined to follow the path of his heart fearlessly to the bitter end, did not find his way to the heart of a people ready for fulfillment but veered almost at a right angle just before the goal, to begin his ascent to heaven. Theocentric thinking repeatedly pulled him back from the final conclusion: like few others of his time, Luther saw the harmful behavior of usury, which the Jews considered their trade; with harsh words, he denounced the Jews as spirits of deceit and betrayal! And yet his anti-Semitism was very superficial, for through baptism as true penance, the Jew could be admitted into the community of the saints! And the Old Testament, with Moses, the patriarchs, and the prophets, remained for him a source of pure closeness to God. Yahweh's voice, spewing from the wilderness into the world, was for him the sole valid law, by which all "human decrees" were deemed devil's work.

From Luther comes the blunt, yet German, saying:

"Trust no fox on the green heath,
Trust no Jew upon his oath,
Trust no pope upon his conscience,
You'll be deceived by all three!"

The vigorous, direct life knowledge of the man was diverted to the heavens! It is a terrible image of German self-destruction to see Luther—the man of the German word—holding the lute in rough peasant hands and singing chorales in honor of Yahweh:

"Holy is God, the Lord Zebaoth,
His honor has filled the whole world!"

Let us contrast this with Hütten's words:

"If only one would recognize,
For the good of the land,
How well it is
That I am called an enemy of the priests!"

Here Hütten addresses the nation:

"Once I wrote in Latin,
Which not everyone understood,
Now I cry out to the fatherland!"

There is no regard for Yahweh's predetermined grace plan, no praise of His power; instead, defiance cries out its rebellious confession into the night:

"Truth must come forth for the good
Of the fatherland. That is my courage.
No other cause nor reason,
So I have opened my mouth!"

Here, law and justice are proclaimed in the name of the nation!

"Alone I have done everything for the benefit and good of the fatherland. Truth drives me. I cannot abandon it, and I have never received any reward for it—indeed, I have suffered more harm. Danger and hardship are my only gains!"

The imperialist of the Cross, the Pope in Rome, certainly hates the renegade monk Luther and despises the Wittenberger, who is filled with an early nationalism, a first instinct of blood. But in Luther and his followers, he can hope that time, under the guidance of his strategists, will again work for Yahweh. Hütten, however, he must destroy for the dangerous example of independent freedom, for his refusal of crutches! It cannot be allowed for the daemons of the North to restore the light-bringer Lucifer to the throne and disrupt Yahweh's world plan. A Luther can be slaughtered or scorched in a grand show trial for the glory of God and to deter the fearful. A Hütten, however, must be made to disappear quietly! Soon enough, Hütten laments secret assassination attempts by the priests against him.

Luther became popular because he could provide his followers and supporters with a final reassurance in the Messiah and heaven. Hütten remained alone because he demanded the ultimate sacrifice from his loyal followers: the solitude of freedom.

"For until now, the Germans are blind.
I urge them to open their eyes,
So that the whole crowd might see
The deceit and cunning of Rome
And how the shepherd tends his sheep
And cares for the salvation of their souls,

How heaven is sold to us,
And God Himself is bartered,
As many a fool runs to Rome
To obtain indulgence and grace.
How the people have been deceived..."

This language was far less tolerable to the imperialists in Rome than the theological attacks of the Wittenbergers. The dialectician Eck could easily overrun the rustic Augustinian Luther with dazzling theology. But against the German sword as wielded by Hütten, the poisonous, angelic tongues of theologians are powerless.

Luther believed in the bodily resurrection; it was a certain comfort to him to think that his finger would grow back in the same, yet purified form after decay and resurrection. He saw this as a special grace in the divine salvation plan, exploring which was the essence of his spiritual life.

Hütten was entirely indifferent to the resurrection; he had no interest in reappearing "one day" in a better afterlife. His only concern was to use his strength to free Germany from the web of the Roman spider. When he spoke of "returning," it was meant very "earthly"—namely, returning in armor, at the head of a liberation army. It's understandable that the third Luther recoiled and fled as if carried off in a cloud! When Hütten even offered to gather an army to drive out all the priests of the world, Luther had to shield his head!

Hütten became homeless in his own time, while Luther was celebrated as a liberator in his lifetime and held in high esteem by many princes. Luther dined with wealthy people, while Hütten, begging, sick, and shivering, staggered past peasant huts.

Melanchthon celebrated himself as the leading figure of the Reformation, gave lectures, traveled to prominent cities and scholars, and involved himself in high-level politics, while the terminally ill Hütten could hardly find a scrap of paper to send a last greeting to the future Germany of his spirit.

And yet, Hütten is the only survivor of his time!

After Luther's sudden death, the Wittenberg theologians under their teacher Melanchthon had prosperous days. Clerical bickering, petty jealousies of narrow-minded intellectual merchants, and all-knowing presumption triumphed. Lutheran orthodoxy fully buried the national heritage that had emerged from Luther's initial rebelliousness. Melanchthon ensured that the Schmalkaldic

League became a mere alliance of interests for certain particularist princes. Wherever ideas of freedom arose, Melanchthon was directly or indirectly on the side of the gravediggers. The bold rebel Wullenwever, who seized power in Lübeck to renew the strength of the Hanseatic League and establish a northern kingdom, ultimately fell due to Melanchthon's intrigues, as Melanchthon could not resist personally interfering in Lübeck's revolt. Wullenwever was betrayed by the "Evangelicals," handed over to the Archbishop of Bremen, and then to the Duke of Brunswick, a fanatical Catholic who had personally tortured Thomas Müntzer, and was illegally executed at Wolfenbüttel.

The Wittenbergers did not lift a finger, and Luther remained silent as Wullenwever's head rolled in the sand at Wolfenbüttel and his tortured body was broken on the wheel.

No one moved a finger as the rebellious peasants, who looked to Wittenberg in desperation and awaited Luther's word, were slaughtered by the thousands. Luther's only word to the peasants—that they should be beaten to death like rabid dogs—squeezed a cry of hatred from the lips of the desperate.

Thus it is: because Luther missed his great national moment, because he trusted Melanchthon more than Hütten or even the far less significant Sickingen, German rebellion dissipated into the sand. The most precious blood was spilled in vain. The German cause fizzled into isolated undertakings. The devastating fanaticism of the Anabaptists was as much a reaction to Wittenberg's failure as the Peasants' Revolt. Luther had already become so spiritually insecure that he retreated to the shaky ground of the Bible whenever one of the fanatics or activists sought a discussion with him.

Rome could smile: the German uprising had been defused! A few centuries later, over the bridge of compromise that Melanchthon built with his Augsburg Confession, Protestantism—having by then betrayed even the last drop of Luther's German blood—could begin its retreat to Rome and its victorious imperialism.

Ignatius of Loyola called for a crusade against the rebellious North to eradicate the last seeds of the Germanic imperial idea that had reawakened in Hütten. When his emissary Lanisius set foot on northern soil, he encountered no spiritual resistance. The Protestants could only counter his approach with their pitiful chorales. The weapons were wielded by power politicians! But these fought for goals other than spiritual ones! The idea of the Reich was buried for a long time beneath the hills of the slain.

The German eagle of freedom that had once soared before Hütten into the heights of the idea of an earthly realm was torn apart by a "Lanisius," a dog.

In 1917, when the weakling on the German imperial throne, under papal pressure, lifted Bismarck's ban on the Jesuit order, the Jesuits, with knowing smiles, returned and named their first establishment after Lanisius, the dog!

Hütten's struggle, in both its origins and its development, is marked by a magnificent inevitability. There is nothing half-hearted, timid, or fearful in him. There is only idea, love of truth, and fiery daring.

In Hütten, a modern man emerged who made himself a torch of truth. He stands among the still limited ranks of true Germanic individuals of this world as a pure German, close in spirit to Dietrich of Bern.

What an untamable fire must have burned within this body, weakened and hollowed by sickness and deprivation, that his soul was able to outlast the abandonment of names that once meant entire worlds: Crotus Rubianus, his friend of youth, fearfully went his own way; Mutian, the once-idolized teacher, retreated into his purely intellectual world; Pirckheimer, the wealthy patrician of Augsburg, slammed the door in his face in outrage when Hütten, who desired nothing but to be entirely German, sought him out; Reuchlin, for whom Hütten had once zealously fought against the obscurantism of the priests and their ally, the baptized Jew Pfefferkorn, shrank away in fear from Hütten's call to arms. Erasmus knelt before the Cross in Rome and eagerly swore to have no association with Hütten, the German revolutionary. Luther turned away in indignation from Hütten's German passion. Melanchthon agitated against him. Sickingen died after an honorable fight and believed in Hütten, his friend, though he did not understand him!

Yes, it was very lonely around the dying Hütten! But when unknown grave diggers at a long-forgotten place on the small island of Ufnau in Lake Zurich dug the shallow grave where they laid Hütten's coffin, the spirit of this revolutionary entered the hearts of the solitary and yearning, giving them the certainty that the realm of this world is eternal as long as men step forth to fulfill their longings.

The third Hütten, as he elevated his struggle to the quintessential German ideal, became the most dangerous explosive for all enemies of this world's freedom and the brightest torch for all the young who set out to find their hearts and, thus, their nation.

What is heaven with its supposed immortality next to the true eternity of the idea of the realm of this world?

What are the saints and the pious of Yahweh's kingdom compared to the true lords and heroes of the North, whose clear light shines brighter, more penetrating, and more enduring than the fiery splendor of Sinai!

Dietrich of Bern found his German singers. His first successor in the idea of the realm, in boldness, in hate, and in love, he found in Ulrich von Hütten, whose memory was desecrated just as the tomb in Ravenna was desecrated!

The Schmalkaldic League was the beginning of the end for the Reich of that time—a Reich that, far from Theoderich's bold plans, was once founded by Karl and was steered like a rotting ship through the turbulent seas of chaotic times by often pitiful crown-bearers at great sacrifice to its substance and honor.

The Emperor was still seen as the frequently unworthy, but nevertheless enduring head of this conflicted Reich. To rise against the Emperor was also to rise against the fragile unity of the fractured Reich, painstakingly preserved and threatened from all sides. The higher the princes raised their heads, the lower the Emperor's esteem fell, and the greedier the lurking enemies became.

The chaos that began with the Reformation allowed the princes to elevate their own power politics to unforeseen heights. The Thirty Years' War, to Rome's delight, left hardly any trace of a visible German Reich. Through the mouth of its legate Aleander, Rome had already declared at Worms that it would respond to any German attempt to break free from Christian politics by driving the thorn of discord into German flesh.

It was a bitter consequence that, instead of Hütten, it was Luther who could stamp his spiritual will on the Reich of his time. No religion can sustain an empire; only a fanatic will can do that. A nation is fed by action, not by prayer! That is Hütten's legacy.

Luther gave the German people a cuckoo's egg: the Holy Scriptures of the Jews!

No one would deny Luther the merit of having taken a great step toward unifying the language of the nation with his German translation of the Bible—the example of Hütten, who wrote in German, had deeply impressed him. However, theologically influenced circles greatly exaggerate when they claim that Luther was the creator of the German written language.

But one fact is often overlooked or obscured: Luther, through the Trojan gift of a "German" Bible, imposed a Jewish framework on the German mindset of his time—so thoroughly, in fact, that for many years, the entire public and intellectual life of the nation was seen and judged, as it were, through the Jewish lens of the Bible. Reformation-era literature is filled with Jewish wordplays, imagery, and examples. The Holy One of Israel became the focal point of all Reformation theology. Luther, the rebel against Peter and the Roman Church of law, inevitably became a follower of the even more dangerous and "Jewish" Paul. The Pauline mode of thinking that awoke in Luther, with its rabbinic and Jewish background, led him to establish a very flexible "Church of Conscience."

This "Church of Conscience" of Protestants in all its variations opened the door wide to hypocrisy. Every ambitious man, every vain priest, every glory-seeking statesman could appeal to their "conscience" to mask their impulsive, personal motives. Such a "Church of Conscience" had to inevitably carry the seeds of disintegration. Followers of the countless sects, in their honor—and to the delight of Yahweh—split each other's skulls to preserve the "purity" of the Jewish message hidden in the Bible. It was a ghastly spectacle to witness how the "purest" Bible scholars—those who took the "uninterpreted" word seriously—also became the most "Jewish." Where law is displaced by "grace," arbitrariness arises. Hence, among "Protestants," there was often a lax attitude toward duty, for after all, "everything is in vain"! The villain might stand high in God's grace, perhaps even higher than the just, so be cautious about premature judgment! The specter of "grace" eliminated the last certainty! When the sense of predestination was added to the concept of grace, the conditions were set for general fatalism. This led to the political principle of "resist not evil," which was fulfilled to the point of national self-destruction. We should never forget that it was evangelical theologians like Dehn and Tillich who opened the doors to Bolshevik subversion. An arch-theologian of watered-down liberal Protestantism, Karl Barth, became a prime witness to the almost wanton submission of the "Word" to any spiritual parasite.

For the Germanic spirit, overcoming the Church of Rome was ultimately easier than overcoming the Church of Conscience!

The coarse Luther, in a tragic twist, became the savior of spiritual Judaism, much as Paul once had.

Consider that in later conflicts, Peter and Paul once again faced each other. Ignatius of Loyola, the bloodthirsty fighter of the Roman Church, fought for Peter; Luther's followers fought for Paul! The fact that German blood flowed in endless streams on both sides must have pleased King Yahweh, whose kingdom of heaven has only ever been seriously threatened by the Germanic people. Yahweh and his representative were the only ones who knowingly, with a smirk, watched the killing, recognizing that both Peter and Paul wanted only one thing: to lead the world under Sinai!

Luther's ultimate conclusion, which cannot be ignored despite his national leanings, was: "Lord, not as I will, but as you will." The Lord, however, is Yahweh, the Lord Zebaoth, and as Luther wrote, there is no other God beside him, and he shall retain the kingdom!

The total Christian worldview of the Middle Ages was not, as the best of his time hoped, replaced by a purely Germanic national one through Luther, but rather split apart!

That was Rome's triumph and the downfall of the fractured Protestantism. Luther may have burst open the sluices of the great Christian reservoir, but he could not channel the waters. Instead, he, himself an immovable rock, stood in the way of the future, dividing the waters so they flowed in two directions: one earthly, the other heavenly. The earthly path was marked by the brilliance of the liberated human spirit, which found purpose, challenge, and fulfillment in science and ultimately in technology. The heavenly path, however—the longing of the unfreed soul—remained confused, chaotic, and lost itself in a maze.

Luther was unable to overcome the theocentric way of thinking! That is his downfall! This is the reason why, ultimately, he must yield to someone greater—namely, Hütten—even if his theological defenders "protest" against it.

Rome may have irreparably divided body and soul in its assessment, yet it united them in service to Yahweh by completely subjugating both and only allowing reason, the mind, to exist as a servant of theology. Luther fully accepted this Christian foundation but granted the mind greater freedom. Thus, over the course of Protestantism's post-Lutheran development, the decisive struggles took place between mind and soul, with the outcome that, by the end of Protestantism's development, the mind could be seen as the soul's adversary!

Rome declared: here is the Pope, here is the Emperor! — and demanded supremacy. Luther divided: here is God, here is conscience, here is the world! — and ultimately gave validity to each. This ended in chaos. The homeless soul of the "Protestants," bound almost in Promethean torment between heaven and earth, could not find a new home even through the brave explorations of the "soulless" mind, so that the mind itself could become materialistic—"godless."

Indeed, one might almost assert that, after Luther, a "bibliocentric" way of thinking emerged in Protestantism, precisely that thinking for the sake of interpretation, which brought about complete stagnation of the soul until the soul's values were ultimately devalued by the mind. Not church or nation, but secularism—that is Luther's end. Not church or state, but state-church—that is the death of the Protestants and the birth of the "Evangelicals."

The principle of authority in church governance that Luther established gradually turned into a farce until it descended into foolishness, as when the last German Emperor donned the clerical robe as "summus episcopus" of his church and delivered a sermon in Jerusalem! This was something an emperor dared to do in the era of Bismarck and Nietzsche!

In light of the development he initiated, Luther can only be regarded as an experiment—a failed experiment! The explosive force Luther devised did not shatter Yahweh's kingdom but the realm of this world!

From the shattered fragments of the Reich, strong rulers of the North attempted to piece together new partial realms. The strength of "faith" in the biblical sense proved to be brittle and, often, hypocritical after the death of the great conqueror Gustavus Adolphus of Sweden, who was a better statesman than an evangelical Christian. A healthy doubt in the power of the gospel of grace arose, and the men of the North longed for the more honest gospel of action.

If the supposed struggle for pure doctrine had turned the world of the North into rubble, then action was to displace death. From this yearning, readiness emerged first in the fiercely contested area of northern Germany. Prussia, the land of the hardest will, arose! Prussia became practically the stronghold of the immortal law, which flourished despite all enmities.

The Brandenburg heartland, that sandbox whose inhabitants had to muster an incredible boldness simply to affirm their meager existence, betrayed by the Roman creature, Count Adam of Schwarzenberg, defied the doom decreed by all forces of darkness and, led by an almost jubilant will to power, rose to the highest heights among the bravest of nations!

Brandenburg-Prussia became an example of what a small people can achieve by mobilizing its will—note well, the soul of Prussia was delivered by neither Rome nor Wittenberg. It grew from the will to live!

What did Frederick William, the future Great Elector, have in terms of external resources when he took power at twenty? His father, George William, a physical and moral ruin, left him with nothing. No money, no administration, no army, no reputation—not even a respectable name! And that miserable father certainly hadn't been able to pursue his own politics. He was nothing more than a pawn of the powerful, an unfree man, driven helplessly into the net of Roman schemes by Schwarzenberg. Is it any wonder that the young ruler began his reign with very mixed feelings? Is it any wonder that he was wracked with disgust at the thought of Brandenburg, a land ravaged by the murderous pestilence of priesthood, looted by marauding mercenaries, and enduring the unspeakable hardships inflicted by Christian Swedes?

Yet the true rulers of the North have always grown by overcoming the greatest difficulties. They grew close to the heart of the secret nation for the burdens and trials they bore for freedom.

Having learned from the crushing experiences his father endured with so-called alliance policies—policies that in essence were merely a weakening of his own will—Frederick William firmly resolved that there could only be one course of action for him: the policy of relying on his own strength and the validity of his own conscience, his own responsibility. Should he submit to the Poles, who held sovereignty over the former Teutonic state, the Duchy of Prussia? Or should he attempt negotiations with the Spanish, the Dutch, and the Swedes to spare the lands of Cleves?

Frederick William knew that politics was impossible without a sword. So he set out to forge that sword, to build an army. The sword of politics, as his warrior blood told him, must be of one piece, not assembled from disparate parts. It could not be allowed for wills other than the ruler's to exist within the army. Apart from duty, no other ideas could reign within an army if it was to be ready for deployment at any moment!

With a fervor that astonished his opponents, Frederick William set about raising an army literally from the ground up. From the soil of his homeland, from the sandy ground of the Mark of Brandenburg, whose men were as tough and unyielding as their pine forests.

He drove out Schwarzenberg, the puppet of the Habsburgs, who at all times denied blood and obeyed Rome, and listened to the wise counsel of the incorruptible Burgsdorff, an enemy of the Pope's policies.

The concentration of forces required, above all, the limitation of hostilities, so he initially replaced false peace treaties with safe ceasefires that served to prepare for harder offensives. After he succeeded in obtaining the investiture with Prussia, Frederick William decided, at first, to forego control of the Oder estuaries and Pomerania in favor of the Swedes at the end of the Thirty Years' War.

All the more determinedly did he proceed, during this "time of peace" that followed, to train and educate his army and the administrative apparatus. Mercenary leaders, along with their bands, were "socialized"—that is, made into state officials and officers. This was a bold undertaking, as only the wealthiest lands—Austria, Sweden, France—could afford standing armies. Yesterday, the world laughed at the Brandenburgers; today, it was forced to acknowledge, with gritted teeth, the superiority of will over the power of wealth.

The Great Elector did not consider asking his country's estates for approval every time he needed funds for rearmament. He resorted to indirect taxes! Thus, in the best sense, he became a socialist, as he placed the burdens of rebuilding the nation upon the entire population for the common good and ensured that the rich, who consumed much, were taxed many times more than the less fortunate. His predecessor had still held to the common notion that the poor should bear much and the rich little! Additionally, Frederick William committed to the necessity of economic planning.

The total integration of the state with his will was, for him, a prerequisite for success. The more isolated and misunderstood he became, the clearer and more determined he was in implementing his plans. He knew no "impossible"— at most, he only knew "not yet."

He had learned the bitter word "wait," a word that had broken many capable but undisciplined statesmen. He allowed his heart to be fueled by comforting hatred—hatred against the "liberating" Sweden that had become a true cancer, prolonging war indefinitely for war's own sake and selling itself first to Austria, then to France, one moment to Luther, the next to the Pope.

Because the Empire had become prey to the cross and its obedient forces, Frederick William recognized the necessity of occasionally having to act in a "small-German" manner to preserve a healthy core for a future, larger Germany.

The policy of a "healthy core" was later pursued even more drastically by Frederick the Great, and Bismarck's vision for the Reich was also "small-German," without, however, betraying the larger Germany.

Frederick William became a master of the politics of the "right moment"—a politics of success that only an autonomous and internally stable statesman can achieve. The prerequisite for such a politics of success is the absolute obedience and resolute will of all true forces of the state—that is, soldiers and officials alike must be not only correct subjects but, above all, ready and committed followers.

The fact that the Great Elector could not only hold together his fragmented lands but weld them into a unified will is a powerful testament to the correctness of his authoritarian thinking. Through him, the history of Brandenburg-Prussia became an example of the victory of small but energy-filled states over far larger but "liberally" led ones.

The Great Elector was often labeled "unfaithful" by democratic chatterers. His loyalty was devoted solely to the higher goal of the state's greatness and security. For this higher loyalty, he broke many a treaty, many an assurance, many a promise, and even many a word. Yet, in the history of nations, a proud breach of word that brings freedom has always been more convincing and manly than a cowardly "faithfulness to treaties," chaining one to a state of servitude. Petty and fearful philistines lack the necessary perspective—the greatness of character—to judge men who break promises for the sake of higher loyalty. The rebels who boldly turned the state's helm in a dangerous moment and saved the nation had to reckon with the possibility that, if their endeavor failed, they would lose not just their heads but also their honor and reputation. All the greater, then, was their courageous play, their daring stakes.

With immense energy, Frederick William set about enlightening his people, preparing them for the ethical concept of a shared destiny. This understanding of the conditions of national unity was meant to enable the state's citizens to make even greater sacrifices and show deeper commitment to all aspects of public life.

This spiritual mobilization was all the more crucial because the Great Elector understood that his land would have to endure countless entanglements and probably many wars to achieve the necessary internal and external unity. The statement, "Remaining neutral is like a worm that devours itself," coined by the great Brandenburg leader, became the fateful motto of his country, which was destined to be the bearer of national unrest in the dying German Empire.

It became Prussia's destiny and national mission not to remain neutral but henceforth to be the seed of all renewal movements within the Empire. When shortly before the Wars of Liberation in 1813 a Prussian king—a weakling on the throne of duty—attempted to stay neutral and defended against breaking imposed alliances for the sake of minor loyalty to the unscrupulous conqueror Napoleon, he came dangerously close to betraying the greater loyalty—a betrayal that might have plunged not only Prussia but the entire German Empire into eternal darkness.

Frederick William knew that a policy of a strong heart must also be a policy of a strong arm. "Alliances are good, but one's own strength is better!" This was one of the realizations that repeatedly led Prussia from humiliation back to the light of freedom.

The Great Elector's efforts to make his land formidable and untouchable through spiritual mobilization, always accompanied by an upswing in all areas of life, are evident in a pamphlet he had distributed throughout the land. Here, Germans were reminded that their ancestors had once been terrifying to the entire world! The appeal was directed at German dynamism, at the passionate arousal of all the blood-based, spiritual, racial values resting and fermenting in the genetic heritage.

It is easy to guess the type of German that the Great Elector—who believed himself to be a Christian—envisioned. At least, he did not imagine the German of his choice as a serious Christian! The line of intellectual ancestors of this great rebel leads back to Dietrich von Bern!

Thus, the Red Eagle of Brandenburg soared high into the skies, causing enemies to tremble. Even if not all of the Elector's plans succeeded, his most crucial plan did: Brandenburg-Prussia became the very idea of the struggle for freedom! Brave men of German blood and Northern spirit came from all over Europe to Berlin to serve under the rising Red Eagle.

Sweden was finally able to be decisively defeated, even if the fearful "world" deprived the Great Elector of the fruits of victory. It is no wonder, then, that thoughts of vengeance, retribution, punishment, and payback did not leave the aging, decidedly un-Christian Elector in peace and drove him from one bold endeavor to the next, even bolder one. Everything suggests that, after dealing with the plundering Swedes, France was to receive the decisive blow, followed by settling accounts with the Emperor, who had become Rome's henchman and saw in the Elector the most dangerous Northern heretic of the time.

The Heretic Prince dared to invite noble and educated heretics, insurgents, rebels, and agitators of Northern blood from all lands into Brandenburg-Prussia—not only to harm the obscurantists or to support the needy in Christian charity, but, above all, to give the land itself a powerful boost by bringing in noble blood and intellectual assets. This brought an ever-growing spirit of productivity to the austere Brandenburg, to Pomerania, and to Old Prussia. Prosperity grew from the sand. This was a tremendous fruit of a will for this world and a faith in this world!

Brandenburg-Prussia became, above all, a haven for freedom of the mind, and the universities, under the Great Elector's protective hand, soon outshone all places of darkness where belated scholastics practiced their dim spiritual craft.

Proud was the land of the Red Eagle, spreading its wings and flying as far as the coast of Guinea! The true lord of this land could proudly counter the unreason that repealed the so-called Edict of Nantes—bringing about the persecution of all freedom-loving heretics in France—with the Potsdam Declaration, which offered sweet solace and a welcoming homeland to all those persecuted for the sake of freedom, truth, and justice.

Certainly, the life of this Great Elector was not without imperfections, as seen in the less-than-ideal execution of some of his plans. Indeed, he may have lacked, in some respects, the ultimate hardness. But his critics should consider that, amid the downfalls of his era, the Great Elector accomplished a unique mobilization of his people's spirit, with nothing else to place on the scales of world history but the concentrated force of a determined will. The fact that this force proved decisive marked the beginning of Prussia's message to the world—the message of duty, honor, and will, the only message that holds authority in the homeland of the strong.

Through Friedrich Wilhelm, the North became, for the first time after a disgraceful period, the pole of freedom once more. For the first time in a land of the North, in Brandenburg-Prussia, a defiant language was spoken again. Even the sacred word "hatred," which Christianity had sought to erase from the lexicon, once again crossed the lips of proud men. For the first time, the empty phrases about so-called "happiness" faded away.

The extraordinary rise of the new Prussia—strengthened through canal construction, drainage projects, the establishment of mills and industries, land improvement, the building of a fleet, the formation of a powerful army, and an unparalleled economic policy—did not aim to provide a happy and content existence for its inhabitants. Rather, it served exclusively the freedom, honor, and greatness of the state, whose sole, yet overwhelming, morality was duty.

Service became the highest command of duty, and it enveloped, seized, and compelled all members of the state—all classes, all people: the Elector, the chamberlain, the officer, the soldier, the official, the farmer, the craftsman, the merchant, and the independent trader. This was the first true socialism, the expression of life and proof of love for the real kingdom of this world.

In the new Prussia, for the first time since Hütten, the German spirit rose again and created the only true German state: a unity of leadership and people bound by a shared duty to a common goal. This state, however, was fundamentally aristocratic at its core: the will of the leader shaped the face and soul of his followers.

The actions of the Great Elector left a lasting influence on Prussia, even when his successor, Frederick I, who elevated Prussia to a kingdom, allowed the army—and thereby the guarantor of freedom—to weaken. The message of duty prevailed over the opulence that was so foreign to Prussian values, which the new king displayed to match the splendor of his "peers." Men like Danckelmann continued to uphold the spirit and will of the Great Elector within their own hearts.

The second King of Prussia, Frederick William I, fully embodied the now-codified Prussian ideal. Luxury, pomp, and indulgence vanished in an instant. The favorites, sycophants, courtiers, intriguers, flatterers, and charlatans fled from the re-militarized Prussia. The strict discipline, the sacrifices made for the sake of the goal, and voluntary austerity as a mark of utmost duty became expressions of the Prussian ethos, giving Europe a new vision. This physically small land raised an army of an unheard-of strength for its time: eighty thousand men. The spirit of Rome had to yield to the military resurgence; in 1734, the witch trials were abolished. Seventeen thousand Protestants arrived from Salzburg alone, seeking refuge in the free Prussian North.

In one respect, however, Frederick William I did not follow the Great Elector: he failed to recognize the inherent disloyalty of the Habsburgs. Serving Rome, the Habsburgs sought to prevent the rise of the North and repeatedly set traps for the king, into which he trustingly fell, leading his people to suffer significant losses in blood and, ultimately, territory.

Yet the "Spirit of Potsdam," the Prussian revelation of law, the military expression of the northern disposition, preserved its superior assurance, pride, and austere severity even in times of disappointment. It did not submit meekly!

Only from this spirit could the living embodiment of the new, warrior-like, and knowledgeable North be born: Frederick the Great!

His youth serves as a remarkable lesson in the inescapable determinism of the northern spirit, which compels the strong to become bearers and fulfillers of law. Frederick, with every fiber of his passionate, beauty-craving heart, rebelled against the Prussian ethos. The merciless demands of duty, which rejected all cosmopolitan and non-military pursuits, drove him to the brink of despair about the meaning of existence. His rebellion was so profound, born from the depths of a soul yearning to escape the rigid compulsion of duty and ascend to the serene heavens of enjoyment, that desertion—even treason against the principles of his state—seemed to young Frederick the lesser evil.

It's understandable that all those in Potsdam and Berlin who were weary of Prussian discipline, as well as those who saw Prussia's demands on individuality and the subordination of personal desires to the common good as oppressive, supported the young Frederick in his rebellion. Above all, the many covert enemies of the freedom of the North, the agents of Rome-bound powers and nations, saw in Frederick's dissent an opportunity. Their calculated support aimed to detach the soul of the heir to the throne from the discipline of law, make him unsteady, and weaken his resolve through unchecked indulgence.

This was a cunning, devious scheme: they hoped a Prussian would become the murderer of the law itself! A man, blindfolded by design, would wield the dagger, convinced of the rightness of his cause.

The forces of darkness, the supranational powers—the Rome-bound and Freemasons, with their cold gaze seeking points of vulnerability in the young prince's soul and wielding the means to exploit them—battled to ensnare the heir's soul. Anything that could erode his strength, character, sense of honor, and self-respect was used as poison. It's an old tactic: to encourage existing desires to grow unchecked, until they become vices, turning the individual into a tool of policy. And then, when the tool is spent, to discard it, leaving it exposed to the curses or laughter of history.

The law had to contend with these forces in its battle for the heir's soul. As is known, the forces of darkness nearly succeeded. Had Frederick managed to flee Prussia, it's likely Prussia would have become a brief yet bright episode in the northern fight for freedom.

It is a powerful and awe-inspiring testament to the unyielding resolve of the law embodied in Frederick William I that he ordered the execution of his son's noble, loyal friend, Katte, and forced the crown prince to witness it. In such moments, souls are either hardened or broken. After agonizing torments, young Frederick's soul ultimately found its path back to the law.

A monument beyond all religions: a king struggles for his son so that the son's soul may become royal as well. He uses the harshest and most ruthless means—a sacrifice of the ultimately innocent and noble. Such a means can only be employed by a true king without staining his soul.

The father's deep love is evident in the records of the crown prince's trial. These records detail every careful precaution the king took to mold his son for the Prussian kingship. He would rather have killed his own son than watch him become a traitor to the Prussian law. Could a king act in a more royal way? And is not the sacrifice of the best precisely what is needed to provide the people with a great, strong, and incorruptible leader?

One thing is certain: Katte, through his sacrifice, became an ever-present reminder of duty throughout Frederick's life. Through his sacrifice, Katte turned a dreamer inclined toward softness into a warrior.

This was a truly royal act: ending the race between law and temptation with the bloody sacrifice of a courageous man. With this act, King Frederick William I. etched his name into the enduring book of history, the legacy of great souls. His name will shine even if, in millennia, the edifices of Prussia crumble and vanish. Through this act, the king led his son out of opposition and into a new role within the Prussian state—a sword stroke that severed the fine web connecting him to the courts of the world, except for Potsdam and Berlin.

A state like Prussia could only survive and thrive through the mobilization of all military strength and the elimination of all weakening, distracting forces. Balancing precariously, Prussia had to avoid any risky experiments as it had come to understand its own laws with clarity. It is idle to question who suffered more during those dark hours: the old king, who saw Prussia and his ideals threatened, or the young crown prince, whose soul cried out at the friend's loss and the complicity it imposed on him, causing him to question his father's humanity.

A whole world of joy, culture, poetry, music, religion, and merriment—carefully nurtured by Prussia's enemies—opened before young Frederick, seeking to trap him and keep him forever. Yet Katte's shadow became the gatekeeper, preventing Frederick from leaving the realm of duty and the revelation of the law.

Against the shadow of Katte, the whispers of pacifist Christian doctrines and otherworldly ideals fell apart. The more isolated the crown prince became, the clearer his understanding and knowledge of the law grew, and the more heroic his realism became.

To reach this realism, he had to navigate the intricate web of intrigue, espionage, and bribery. Even the queen, due to Prussia's precarious position between the Western powers and Habsburg—both of whom secretly despised Prussia and sought to use it to their advantage—was caught up in conspiratorial circles. She thought more in line with Western ideals, contrary to the king, and accepted financial support from those powers in exchange for information, which amounted to espionage.

From his earliest youth, the crown prince had to endure profound tests of soul and character, compounded by physical challenges when the king insisted he undergo rigorous military training to counteract the softening influences of opposition. The planned escape from duty's constraints into the rosy semblance of freedom ultimately became an escape from rebellion against the law into the true life of duty. This defied France's plan, which aimed to ensnare the prince politically by indulging his desires. Enraged, the French ambassador, who was playing a very risky game with the prince's soul, nearly urged his bribed court allies to stage a coup against the old king.

Yet the King of Prussia proved stronger than the powers of darkness. It's worth noting that this old king was naturally a kind-hearted man who, knowing himself as the bearer of the Prussian law, did not shy away from the harshest severity to uphold the commandment of duty. Thus, the old king became the founder of a discipline that only the North truly understands, which hostile forces disparaged as mere "bootlicking."

In the old king arose the great third way, beyond the Western liberalism veiled in pacifism and cosmopolitanism, and beyond the Eastern, submissive mentality prone to the lash and enduring servitude: he elevated duty as the highest law of life. The foundations of this spirit and character revelation, laid by the Great Elector, became systematized under him.

England, France, and Habsburg Austria could send their sons out into the wide world to find their place, face trials, and rise; Prussia, however, confined its sons to the narrow, joyless daily grind—to the barracks and the drill grounds. And by doing so, Prussia achieved an unparalleled concentration of will, which had to be gathered, controlled, and restrained so that, in the hour of need, it could burst forth with overwhelming force. This is the often misunderstood and maligned Prussian law—a force that has, more than once, shaken a deceitful world to its core.

Numerous German principalities drew strength from the influences of a softened and softening West, yet Prussia lived dangerously and modestly, though it lived with awareness, and thus, even in the most troubling times, securely!

1730 marks the year of the crown prince's escape attempt; ten years later, he assumed power. These ten years were a period of new self-formation. This illustrates how vitally important it is to lead young people to points of the hardest decisions through proper education. A knowledgeable and thus valuable person is born only in the moment of decision. The fate of the crown prince proves how misguided and disastrous it is to assign tasks to an undecided person. Whoever loves the youth of their nation should grant them the opportunity for decision-making.

The young king would have faced far more challenging years of searching and struggling on the throne, along with many anxious hours for the state, had the old king avoided the demand for a decision! Katte's death forced the crown prince to choose—either to accept life from the perspective of state reason or to reject it entirely. After this decision, the crown prince used the remaining years before his ascension to power to learn with awareness, forging the deadly sword of a vigilant spirit.

Thus, he became impervious to fate. As a steady and unwavering person, he could master the highest military art—the planning and decision-making, the thinking and command, drawn from the moment. This is the supreme military art of instinct, for which no battle rules or mechanical learning exists.

This is how he could rein in a rebellious, gritting Europe and impose upon it the law of his will.

Thus, he himself became the most powerful instrument of Prussian will, one who, in the truest sense, burned up in service. His way of life became a model. He was thus not only the creator of an authoritarian state but also of an authoritarian person of will.

The warrior spirit mobilizes all forces within a person—of will, blood, and soul—toward the highest achievement, and its stance aims to eradicate all weakening and disintegrating elements. The young Frederick was saved from the dangers of weakening by the law of Prussian duty, which the old king had instilled in him.

The life-affirming warrior perceives all the beauties of existence especially intensely and loves them precisely in his readiness for sacrifice. Yet, he remains master of these beauties, never a slave to their enjoyment. This life intensity grants him heights of perception that the pleasure-seeker, absorbed in daily indulgence, can never attain.

From the Great Elector to the Old King to the Great Frederick, there is a clearly developing path of insight, implementation, and ultimately the realization of the guiding law.

The law of the North, expressed in the highest degree of manliness, in warriorhood, is aimed at cultivating intensity of life. Thus, Frederick also had to become the foremost caretaker of his country and of his devoted people. The peasantry, considered a particularly important class, was placed under the supportive protection of the state. Peasants were no longer to be "laid low"; they were freed from exploitation and oppression. Younger sons of farmers now had the prospect of viable settlement opportunities in the Prussian East, which was opened up and made arable by every means. Jews were not permitted to acquire estates and farms. The interest rate was regulated.

Blow after blow, the shackles hindering a healthy internal development were broken. Torture—a means derived from the era of Christian world domination, used to extract confessions beneficial to the Church and to eliminate anyone deemed unfavorable or dangerous—was abolished. Here too, it proved true that a truly strong state is also always the most magnanimous! Only weakness leads to arbitrariness, oppression, injustice, and violence.

For the first time, the entire legal system was imbued with a German spirit. Lawyers disappeared. A new code of laws, a new, fairer, improved legal process emerged. Frederick's strong state became also the most just in Europe. Instead of the deceitful phrases about human rights, a new order of human duties arose, which alone constitutes a true expression of authentic humanity.

"I do not need to live, but I must act!" This is Frederick's first commandment in the doctrine of the new order of human duties. Here lies the powerful breakthrough of the Germanic attitude through all religions and philosophies of the past Christian or Christian-influenced millennium. This is the rise of the German spirit, the breaking of all mental crusts by the dynamite of concentrated will.

Quietism, Pietism, Optimism, Pessimism—all these terms are rendered powerless by the stance of heroic realism, born from the understanding of law, which Frederick the Great's spiritual successor, Friedrich Nietzsche, developed into one of the most masculine teachings of all time.

Here, for the first time, the free German spirit speaks again through Frederick.

It's no wonder that Frederick became the loneliest figure in Europe!

Even in his bitterest hour, the nobility of his soul shone through the darkness that fate cast around him. As he wrote in a letter from March 1740 to Minister Count Podewils:

"I am only king if I am free. If I fall, my wish is that my body be burned in the Roman manner and laid to rest in an urn at Rheinsberg!"

It is incomprehensible how feeble interpreters dared to tinker with the image of this complete Nordic man, how they presumed to scrutinize every moment of his unique life under a microscope, eager to detect a flaw or a minor crack to proudly report to a scornful, narrow-minded world. Particularly absurd are the attempts from certain quarters to salvage this individual, who had risen above every established religion and worldview and dedicated himself fully to the realm of this world, as a Christian figure after all!

These people, in their foolish audacity, resemble villagers who call fire "dirty" merely because it raises specks of ash!

Shortly before his death, the truly luciferian Frederick was able to say:

"I have always loved the light!"

The light of his stance, which radiated from him, guided thousands of the North's finest to find the way into their own hearts and into the heart of the nation. For Frederick's spirit leads beyond Prussia, which served only as a reservoir for rediscovered or awakened northern energies, into the realm of this world, into a greater Germany!

The gateway to the homeland of the strong was finally opened by Friedrich Nietzsche, who placed the explosive charge of lawful thought against the massive rubble of collapsed systems, edifices, and temples, clearing space for the bold shock troops of the rising new millennium. It was an extraordinarily daring endeavor to translate the breakthrough of principles into words and concepts, into demands, commands, slogans, and proclamations. The language of philosophies and religions was insufficient for this, so Nietzsche created a new, poetic language for his work, which itself became a linguistic marvel.

The so-called intellectual world, trudging along in old pathways, failed to understand Nietzsche's daemonic vision, merely able to stare at it with the resentment that every doomed figure harbors toward the life-affirming, vigorous one who displaces him. Nietzsche's first blow against all "miracles" and random occurrences, from which the fearful and the oppressed derive their spiritual sustenance, was his declaration of the recognition of a higher purpose in all that is strong, emerging, and creative. There is now no thing for its own sake, not even an unbound idea! Not even a god exists for his own sake! The higher purpose supersedes all mere spectator theories of religions, ideologies, and philosophies. The intellectual world, previously enclosed by incomprehensible concepts and dense hedges of erudition, was suddenly thrown open, revealing and clearing away cobwebs and voids.

A new spirit blows in the cold northern winds, freezing many timid hearts and weak souls. Nietzsche begins to judge, to tear down, to overthrow, to permeate, creating space for something seemingly impossible: the new human, the Übermensch, who, through the immense momentum of his own will, elevates the soul to undreamed-of triumphs, even to the ultimate triumph over fear and death.

Amid an environment contented and comfortable, the Übermensch of the purified northern spirit declares commitment to a dangerous life as the only life worth living. In an age tinged with pacifism, the high song of warriorhood without pity resounds. It's understandable, then, that the secure citizenry smiled dimly and shrugged at the demand that freedom, too, has a higher purpose, bound to an ultimate aim. The barren questionings, mere cheap speculation in the end, are overcome by a call for a new relationship with life, for a profound embrace of life's essence.

Zarathustra, the singing, smiling, faithful warrior, a new Lucifer, enters this fear-stricken world with a message that promises death to the weak, but true life to the strong. Whereas, in the pre-Socratic era, the philosopher was the guardian of statecraft and later declined into a theologically infused contemplative thinking, now a new doctrine emerges. This doctrine, implanted as the seed of a new humanity in the heart of the nation, is destined once more to transform educators and statesmen into guardians of the true eternity of this world.

Where Kant established duty as the boundary of moral education, Nietzsche's message calls forth a higher duty and a powerful will. It is no arrogance to say that only the North could give birth to such an idea rooted in law. Once again, the northern lights illuminated the world as suns and moons faded. The dynamite of the Übermensch became the superior spiritual stance of National Socialism; its herald and realizer, the creator of the Third Reich — the Germanic Empire of the German Nation in reality — is spirit of that same spirit. The creator of the myth of the 20th century descends with a perspective from these northern heights: revealing, destroying, and rebuilding.

When gods die, Übermenschen inherit their legacy. This was taught by Prometheus, and this is Zarathustra's testament.

It is no wonder that the gods hide their heads and that the underworld stirs in a storm against the bold, the strong, and the daring who come! A wondrously austere, long-forgotten world re-emerges, growing out of Nietzsche's words and images into a new, purified reality. Not a city with golden gazes, no, but a world full of the clamor of arms and war songs, full of discipline and order—a world of hardness and decency!

The ancients could hardly have envisioned the resurgence of Atlantis more wondrously, nor could the Germanic tribes have imagined the emergence of the new Earth after the great fire more beautifully, than Nietzsche, when he lets Zarathustra carry the new world of the knowing and willing, the prepared and the warrior-like, from the lonely heights down into the valleys of humankind.

The suffering of the ascent, which the Übermensch must endure on his path to the mountain of perfection, is illuminated by the beauty of the royal mantle of a new humanity that will adorn him there. The realization is powerful and more than comforting: suffering serves not to yield to the will of a god but to recognize one's own strength and awaken resistance!

About a hundred years ago, Nietzsche was born, and how thoroughly the world has been transformed by the dynamite of his soul! In the coming era of races and nations, the true worth of this Luciferian thinker will only be fully appreciated, and his value will endure as long as there are conscious nations and proud humans.

The immense burden of spiritual struggle that Nietzsche took upon himself broke him physically and mentally. But no god struck the Übermensch with madness, as some pious minds would have us believe. And, moreover, no heretic would ever renounce their heresy out of fear of heavenly punishment!

How petty are the attempts of those who reject this world of homelands, nations, and races to accuse Nietzsche of an un-German attitude! When Nietzsche uses the whip to spur on the weary, behind all his serious, admonishing, and concerned words stands a great love for people—people whom he wishes, even under unbearable anguish, to lead to the heights. Let those who reject this world search their own ranks for traitors; they would be occupied for a lifetime. And let them leave to the disciples of this world the order of the things, values, and people of this world.

How commanding, defiant, and — believing is Nietzsche's realization that all culture — which the weak-minded might see as the offspring of religion — strives only to create the genius!

The purpose of all creation serves the enhancement of life! This is the purest doctrine of eternity from this world.

What does it matter if the lightning of heaven can strike the defiant rebel on the highest mountain peak? Those who have glimpsed the eternity of this world remain present in this eternity; they cannot die!

Thus, the strong live according to the law that determines the order of their lives. They are no slaves to morality, no servants of fear, but sovereign masters, freed through the knowledge of the true values of humankind, fulfilling creation's ultimate purpose: to bring forth living beings for this world, taking the place of the old gods, like Prometheus once did!

The great awakening of the nation, which also signals the dawn of the rising Germanic race, has proven the validity of Nietzsche's call for the new human being.

Nietzsche stands among the Übermenschen, the true gods of Germania, who not only prevented the downfall of the North but also infused it with a dangerously vibrant spirit.

And this spirit will take on a physical form on the day of the race. That day will be a "Last Judgment," not one held by Yahweh and his followers in the Valley of Jabbok near Jerusalem, but by the Germanic people!

These reborn Germans, born of blood and race, will give the world its face: an open, faithful, and resolute face!

The essence of politics lies in mobilizing the dormant forces and passions within the race to realize the will of the people. This national will awaits its test, awaiting the call of the nation's leader, who grasps the "right moment," as the Greeks called the fateful hour, to dare the history-making action with this will.

The mobilization of these forces and passions is the work of the people's educators—those who are spirit from the eternal spirit of the nation and blood from the eternal bloodline that sustains the true leader.

If the birth of a people is creation, then the education of a people is continuous generation. Woe to the nation that entrusts this generation to those who are otherworldly.

Education of the people is impossible without discerning and valuing history as the judgment of nations. And: whoever senses nothing of the soul's movements within their people will never comprehend the law of nation-building!

Education, then, should be: lifting the people over depths, chasms, and ravines to the heights of a conscious life that follows the lawful rhythms of the racial soul, toward ever-new goals of perfection.

Already, the march of the Germanic columns echoes through the young morning as they set out to find their homeland, never to lose it again. While the old ones feared death, the young heard the call to arms. On the old flag of longing, new symbols of certain hope were fixed. And with hands trembling in eager excitement, the young wrote their own banner's motto:

"One People — One Empire — One Leader!"

The forces of darkness prepare for a final assault to banish this empire from reality forever. They voice their threats.

The young laugh defiantly.

"Punishment of God — Let him punish; we will resist!"

"The power of fate — We will break the dragon of fate with defiant teeth."

"Predestination for downfall — The law is here. It does not predetermine its own end, and the Lord of the World is the enforcer of the law!"

Ancient is the struggle between night and light!

And after the darkest night, has not a bright day always risen? The law cannot be bent!

So then: whoever thinks they can capture the light and bind it into darkness, let them rise and stand in the path of the truth-made-real, the Germanic Empire of this world as it grows toward perfection!

The law kills those who seek to bend it!

CHAPTER

4

THE MATERNAL WOMEN

When the solitary and strong perished in defiant bitterness, the final hour also struck for the maternal women. A weak millennium that condemned the warrior men also had to despise the maternal women—the women who, through their own nurturing strength, helped men find the path to heroism all the more surely, as manhood, elevated by refined purpose, achieves a powerful surge toward the perfect act.

It is an ancient, ever-recurring song of the North: the hero ventures forth, seeking, after the hour of proving himself, after overcoming all trials and dangers, to find the ultimate and greatest experience—woman. The woman for whom it is worth fighting.

Woe to the man who is not strong enough to win a noble woman! If he is weaker than the woman, he will be killed by her or her blood relatives as punishment for his attempt to dishonor a noble woman.

To the noblest man, the noblest woman! This is an ancient northern demand, for which even wars are not avoided, so that the finest bloodlines of the race, in the union of the two noblest, will produce something new, something higher, something greater.

The heroic songs, telling of wild adventures, daring deeds, and hardened hearts, also sing the praises of the waiting, hopeful woman who waits for years for the one to whom her blood calls out with joy.

And there, where a woman is desecrated by deceit, betrayal, or theft by one unworthy, begins the first act of a powerful tragedy that may lead entire tribes to their downfall.

There is in the figure and myth of Kriemhild an intense tribute to an extraordinary woman who suffered injustice because she was bound to an inferior man. Such a woman might even come to despise her own children if she realizes that the man who fathered them is unworthy. Medea, that legendary woman of northern blood, when her captor Jason broke his loyalty and revealed an unheroic character, committed the dreadful act of slaughtering her children and serving their flesh to him, then returned to her old homeland in a dragon-drawn chariot.

Euripides, the great pagan Greek tragedian of northern spirit, gave Medea a monumental depiction in his drama. A bourgeois or even Christian mind can only speak with horror of such exceptional women, whose honor is so deeply connected to the fulfillment of life alongside a superior hero—a life rendered meaningless if, instead of fulfillment, they face betrayal. With lost honor, life itself is lost. Though the dishonored soul may rise once more for a terrible act of revenge, it ultimately fades into darkness after the cup of vengeance is drained.

A degenerate era, which saw in women only objects of unrestrained desire and labeled disgusting, indiscriminate wastefulness as "passion," wrongly accused northern women of cold-heartedness. On the contrary, the northern woman is capable of the highest passions of love and hate, but her passions are deeply anchored within, so that the storms of her soul rarely erupt in loud expressions.

One must never forget that the purest and most passionate song of love, the "Song of Gudrun," the northern Germanic Kriemhild, has no counterpart in world literature—perhaps with the exception of the Odyssey.

What is the so-called Song of Solomon, revered by Jews and Christians, compared to this humanity of the North? A sultry praise of a female's physical charms, which the aging Jewish king Solomon intended to add to his already extensive harem. Throughout all times, German poetry has differed from Jewish and Jew-influenced poetry in that German poetry never reduced a woman to mere femininity, even in the most ardent depictions of love. Indeed, one can and must judge the worth of German poets by the standards with which they regard women.

Amidst the church's persecution of women, which, in its life-destroying doctrine, condemned Eve, the "female," as the vessel of the first and therefore inherent sin, and dethroned the royal woman, the life-giving mother, the minstrels rose to defend womanhood. Walther von der Vogelweide, the greatest political messenger of his time, also became a defender of the honor of the Germanic maternal woman. He does not sing of the "holy" women detached from the world; he praises the German woman!

The noble, dignified women who commit themselves to only one man are worthy of the songs of those traveling, freedom-seeking men. These are proud women, whose foreheads shine with the radiance of superior motherhood, women who once presided in the noble halls of Germanic courts, women in whose presence any impertinent word would fall silent. Such women were heralds of the true eternity of creative life, and to slander a maternal woman was a crime worthy of death.

Only with reverence can we still read the verses of the Odyssey today, which glorify royal women who, alongside men as equals and untouchables, were guardians of justice, home, and people.

Throughout world literature, whenever we encounter laudatory depictions of noble, maternal women, we can observe the influence of the North, of the great Aryan race. For a Jew, it would be utterly impossible to revere such a woman! Even the cult of the Virgin Mary, who, whenever she is mentioned in the "New Testament," is far from being "holy," only enters into the religious ideas of Christianity when it merges with certain Aryan myths.

The women of the "Bible" are, by and large, exceedingly questionable figures, often outright prostitutes like Esther. A singer of the North would never have misused his genius to depict the fate of a harlot. This is also due to the fact that the ethics proclaimed by Northern singers served exclusively the higher purpose of educating the people.

On Sinai dwelt the desert god Yahweh, who resorted to the most impossible means, surrounded by an atmosphere of fear that encouraged all forms of superstition. On the Greek Olympus, by contrast, goddesses sometimes even surpassed the gods. In the land of the Midnight Sun, however, in the high North, the goddesses were flesh and blood!

Just as the gods of Germania were nothing other than "superhumans," heroes who exceeded the common human measure, so too were the goddesses of Germania noble women who thought and acted royally, setting the standard for all women of Germania.

Two creative poles lead to life and its preservation: generation and birth. Disregarding one of these poles would have led to ruin. The Northern person, deeply rooted in life awareness, would never have dared to desecrate one of these poles out of reverence for the law and knowledge of order; he would neither have created an absolute male right devoid of instinct, nor would he have tolerated an Amazonian state.

For the Greeks and Romans, the sun was a male concept. This male creative pole fertilizes the female creative pole, the earth, thus generating the sacred life of nature. The earth is the primordial mother; her womb brings forth what is necessary for the sustenance of the body. Therefore, the primordial mother earth is surrounded by a circle of myths, both idealistic and poetically beautiful.

Measured against the powerful ideas of the Northern realm, Jewish thought, even in its rather pitiful myths, is so materialistic that it does not acknowledge a "Mother Earth." The earth is merely matter to them, nothing more. Hence, this matter can also be cursed by Yahweh, just as Yahweh can fix the sun, as mere matter, like a lantern on the ceiling of the heavens!

One must recognize the immense difference, the unbridgeable chasm between the Northern realm and Sinai: in the North, the sun is a generative force, whereas on Sinai, the sun is merely one of the light sources that Yahweh placed for the benefit of his people. Similarly, the man of Sinai, as a tool of Yahweh's arbitrariness, lacks his own creative will. He lacks the light-bringing, Luciferian, divine quality! The woman of Sinai lacks the divine primal law of birth, and so she inevitably becomes a vessel of lust.

Ungodly, materialistic people crawl through the dust of Sinai—the born materialists! In the North, however, stride noble, divine, knowledgeable people who themselves are part of the eternal law.

Here lies the profound knowledge of the immediate, lawful connection of the Northern person with the universe, the foundation of divine kinship, divine brotherhood. This emerges even in the often unclear expressions of mysticism, pantheism, and fervor, surfacing in thought and action. To the Northern person, God is the crowning of the law: the infinite will to eternal life.

He may be revered in the language of the soul but never beseeched for a "miracle."

The thought of a being who could exist outside the boundless creative rhythm of the law is inconceivable to the Northern mind.

Not "Man or Woman" is the battle cry of the North, but "Man-and-Woman as a Creative Unity" is the command of eternal life in this world.

As long as the North remained law-abiding and knowledgeable, no movements arose that demanded or allowed one part of this creative unity to be less respected. Such insights were too natural, too deeply rooted in instinct. That disagreements over these fundamental premises of life could even arise is already a sign of decline. One should recognize how dangerous, corrosive, and deadly all religions are that do not build upon the knowledge of the law and its life-sustaining demands. It is well known that dogmatic religions only emerge when the harmony of understanding, knowledge, soul, and blood—that is, the genetic heritage of the strong race—has been lost!

Above all, one should also recognize here that there can be no "world religion" any more than there can be a "world culture." Any world religion would presuppose the destruction of races and the complete dilution of nations. It is no coincidence that the most fanatical supporters of world religions are usually also staunch fanatics of racial enmity.

It is also no coincidence that, for example, followers of the Kingdom of Yahweh—whether power-hungry Jews or zealous Christians—harbor a deadly enmity against the strong and the knowledgeable of all peoples. For these strong ones are conscious bearers of an inheritance that resists equalization and, like a magnet, attracts all similarly inclined forces.

Especially the warrior North, the land of duty, the homeland of the strong who embody the law in their order, will restore maternal women, the dethroned queens of life, to their rightful place. The strong, law-conscious, warrior man longs for the maternal woman—not as a toy, but as a companion, a co-creator—for the sake of fulfilling the unity of creation.

The homeland of the strong will be a land of freedom and glory, and thus of true happiness, for the young people rising from this perfected alliance of the two united divine poles.

The strong of this world yearn for maternal women. It is a yearning for fulfillment, which has nothing to do with mere desire.

This marks the end of the "little woman," cast out from the homeland of the strong so that her offensive presence no longer desecrates the sanctity of the maternal woman, who is the bearer of the overwhelming message of the law, the embodiment of the truest proof of life's devoted essence. In the homeland of the strong, there is no place for the courtesan.

Is it really a coincidence that the same pitiful, gutter-minded, spiritless "satirical rags" mock both warriors and women in the same breath? Pacifism not only degrades heroes into contemptible mercenaries; it also desecrates maternal women, reducing them to courtesans.

It is the same spirit of the inferior, fighting for their own realm and rule, that seeks to drag down humanity, dignity, and pride into the dirt until all aspiring life is leveled.

The day is not far when maternal women will once again take their honored place in the hall. With gentle hands, they will soothe the worries of an imperfect everyday life from the brow of the man, the comrade, and the bright, carefree laughter of their children will forever restore his faith in the eternity of his duty. The humanity that grows from this knowing and proud duality will, as in ancient times when myths were reality, be godlike once more!

From the union of these two creative forces emerges the most vital cell of the community: the family, whose life has been and continues to be as strong and life-giving in the Germanic realm as nowhere else in the world. Where else can a child believe so deeply in the purity of its mother into adulthood as in the North?

In the homeland of the strong, there are no "marital problems." Even less are there marital experiments, as favored by times of bourgeois decay. The woman is not to be an experiment, nor the man an experimenter!

The only question in a marriage is whether the two creative forces coming together are truly meant for each other. This requires the most precise evaluation of all values and an assessment of those lesser qualities that, if overlooked, often become obstacles over time, causing the marriage to falter. The happiness of a marriage depends on whether the resonance of the two souls, united in their creative purpose, forms a harmonious chord. The subtle vibrations of the soul should not be drowned out by the loud clamor of mere physical desire.

The path to marriage begins with a child's education, teaching them first to understand themselves—that is, to find the path to their own heart. A person who knows the sound of their own soul and the language of their heart can also hear the essence of their companion. But how can someone find harmony in a partnership if they don't understand their own heart, blood, and soul?

Indeed, mistakes in choosing a life partner may still occur among the strong. Such errors are resolved by separating, allowing each to seek fulfillment in a new union. Such separation happens without hatred. However, for those who are truly united in harmony, their marriage remains indivisible.

Finding this unity is the highest wisdom of marriage.

How distant seem the years when a "marriage of convenience" stood in contrast to a "marriage of love." Both paths, fundamentally, led to ruin. Convenience was equated with money, while "love" implied the absence of duty and responsibility, driven merely by a desire for satisfaction.

Equally distant appear the times when people argued over the "system" for the number of children. Children, seen as a necessary burden, were treated as something not to cause too much work—a dreadful sign of decaying national morality! The maternal womb, the sacred vessel of eternal life, was degraded in the crudest way. Children were no longer the great third entity, the new and better product of a union, but a luxury that, when measured against the comforts of bourgeois life, seemed excessively costly.

One must never forget that these times of decline are always latent, as long as the weak are allowed to spread the pitiful "ideas" of their weakness. If the strong were ever to grow complacent and indifferent, forgetting the dormant dangers that still lurk beneath, the weak would seize power with a single blow, and those vile doctrines would raise their Medusa's head once again.

The homeland of the strong must also be the homeland of the vigilant, meaning the sword must never rust!

As long as the Earth endures, as long as people are born into this world, there will be day and night, the strong and the weak. Only that the strong should hold onto life and dominion aligns with the creative will embedded in the eternal law.

And may the strong find joy in the duty that calls them to sustain, to create, and to nurture life for the sake of eternal life, aided by the loving spirit of maternal women.

A woman who finds fulfillment in motherhood through her creative duty stands above childless women as a hero stands above the followers. No scorn toward women whose wombs remain closed to life should diminish their pride.

What indeed are all the "brides of Christ" together compared to a single maternal woman, who presents her husband with a healthy, laughing child whose eyes reflect a faith in this world? What are all the promised delights of a hallelujah-filled heaven compared to the joy of motherhood, which ignites with the first cry of the child?

Mothers are the true heralds of the splendor of eternal life on this Earth. Anyone who sees the radiant glow in a mother's eyes as she gazes at her newborn, a glow of profound inner joy, has witnessed the light of a hundred suns and a thousand heavens.

No greeting from a "spiritual bridegroom" can outshine the joyful song of the heart when a mother's child reaches out its arms to her for the first time. Thus, mothers are deeply bound in loyalty to their great sister, the Earth.

How can these maternal women do anything but scorn—and at best, pity—all those pitiful "free love" women who seek only to experience pleasure? This same disdain is known only by the strong warrior who, armed and ready, marches toward the decisive moment, only to meet a weakling waving a palm branch.

On the heights of humanity, the strong of this world walk hand in hand with their maternal women. They are the first in the homeland of the strong. The brightness of their gaze is a spark of that eternal fire that burns the weak and purifies the strong to the utmost clarity.

The world becomes beautiful where the homeland of the strong begins. The joyful sound of children's laughter fills this new homeland, a place full of goodness because it knows how to eliminate the unworthy.

And the maternal women keep watch over the cradles of eternity!

CHAPTER

5

DESPITE CURSE & OPPOSITION: THE STRONG!

Space, where the Strong have risen to stride forward with upright gait, eyes fixed on the distant goal, to walk into a life filled with struggle, caring not for gratitude, reward, or punishment. Then come the "scribes," for whom the reality of a greater human freedom does not fit within their doctrine of blind submission, warning of the terrible consequences of "arrogance," which they claim as a sure sign of impending divine retribution.

Indeed, the scribes even pray to this heaven to hurl down a bolt of lightning, to strike the transgressor whose "evil deed" is strength and defiance, to kill him— making him an example of terror for the world of darkness. But the Strong march on, unconcerned by the consequences of their ascension toward greatness, taking the path to fulfillment.

They know that the scribes have drawn a boundary around their own baseness and, in fear of their lowliness being exposed and themselves being cast out, take anxious care to ensure no one crosses it. The Strong know that the scribe can only be overcome by the boldness of courageous deeds, and that it is through such deeds that the boundary is shattered and rendered powerless. They know that their example can instill new strength and confidence in the hearts of those who wait.

Truly, the scribes' lightning strikes do not ignite, nor can they even cause fright. The thunder of their heaven proves to be merely the rustling of paper, and their "lightning" nothing but ink! The magicians, once the tyrants over fearful and superstitious souls, become objects of childish ridicule when their deception is revealed. Thus, a natural enmity exists between the magicians, who spread a veil of deceit over reality to rob and plunder in the twilight, and the Strong, who tear away the deception to dispel the specter with the bright light of the sun.

The Strong know that no god can be mighty in the Weak. Rather, it is the Weak who rely on superstition, magic, and delusion to gain influence meant to nullify the example set by the Strong. What kind of god, then, would raise the Weak above the Strong? Would that not be a god of injustice, one that exists out of fear and, therefore, out of destruction?

Such a god would lead his followers to power along crooked paths! The crooked path proclaimed by the scribes is that of miracles. The Strong do not believe in miracles, for to do so would mean denying the certainty of the law. They do not bow to an arbitrary power that elevates miracles above action, and thus grace above loyalty.

For the sake of loyalty, the Strong prefer to struggle along the arduous path of action, which leads through thorns and dangers to the summit of their goal, rather than allowing themselves—without will—to be carried lightly and effortlessly by an angel of miracles into the whimsy of a despotic god.

The Strong would rather have their skin pricked by thorns if only they can walk the self-chosen path of knowledge with the proud sense of their own strength. The feeling of "owing thanks to no one," even in the limitations of what they have achieved, is far nobler and more beautiful, deeper and more genuine, than the greatest gratitude for effortless grace.

Thus, the Strong do not wish to be granted a heaven of grace. They can only love a heaven they have conquered for themselves.

Therefore, their heaven is the kingdom of this world! Justice is their claim, not grace their prayer!

The homeland of the Strong will be filled with the defiant, the jubilant, the ones who scorn and the victorious. The more venomous the curse of the scribes, the otherworldly, the weak, the harder will be the songs of defiance and the commands of resistance. Even in the hour of deepest despair, the Strong will not trade their freedom for an eternity of convenient dependency and arbitrary grace. Let the otherworldly cross themselves and speak of stubbornness—the Strong know it is only loyalty to the law that binds them to life with all its realities.

Never will the Strong allow themselves to be reconciled with a god who is mighty in the weak, for such reconciliation would mean nothing but a submissive acknowledgment of a power that disregards the will and law of the Strong.

The Strong would rather perish in the storming pursuit of the crown of life than submit cowardly. They do not even desire the crown of victory if it was not earned through their own triumph. Consolation prizes may be welcome to the characterless weak. To the Strong, they are an insult!

The old Frisian saying, "Better dead than a slave," applies all the more in the land of the soul and its yearning, which is the sky above the homeland of the Strong.

A god who delights in broken souls, who seeks to humble the Strong and make them bow to the weak, the cowardly, the pitiful, the will-less, is no brother to the Strong—and even less their lord!

Once again, the scribes rise to proclaim the blessing of the Lord upon all who bow to him. Yet the Strong remain unaffected by any blessing if it is a grant of grace outside the law. If there exists a blessing, it lies in the radiance of the perfection achieved through the fulfillment of the law. This perfection grants a security that rises above all fate—something no blessing or reward can replace or surpass.

If a weakling, due to a life free of struggle and thus of little consequence, manages to wrap himself in the mantle of wealth, mistaking it for the armor of true power and wears this mantle to his last days, he may cheaply have it inscribed on his tombstone that here lies a "blessed one." The Strong merely scoff at such a blessing, which they see as nothing more than a hindrance and burden.

An unbroken heart is worth more than all blessings. Thus, even in misery, the Strong remain mightier than the most blessed of all time. Hutton was powerful; Melanchthon was blessed. Prussia was a mighty land; France, a blessed one. Nietzsche was indeed mighty, but he was not blessed, nor did he wish to be.

A radiant heart is worth more than a halo! For inner radiance is of one's own merit, whereas a halo is merely a loan from heaven. In times of decision, it quickly becomes evident that a radiant heart can uphold a stance far more than the prayers of all the blessed ever could.

The concept of blessing granted only from heaven is often confused with the impact of a perfected being. A "blessed deed" is merely the act of the Strong, which yields an outcome that, in turn, brings forth perfection. Too often, such blessed acts starkly contradict the "salvation will" of those who professionally dispense blessings.

A primary task of the scribes is to portray an obvious effect of the law as a sign of divine blessing, so that the people of an era do not recognize and cheer for a great one but rather bow their knees and piously parrot, "Behold, what a turn by God's providence!"

Frederick the Great understood the impact of the law and mocked his generals' zeal in desperately pleading for heaven's blessing before every battle. For this reason, Frederick was far more faithful than his generals, for in misfortune, where the pious submitted as God's will, he alone retained inner radiance and, with it, a clear vision for what was necessary.

The devout has it much easier than the Strong—this is a consolation, though a rather dubious one, for all the weak. Consolation, the refuge of the weak, is found in the blessing-giving heavens that patiently and unceasingly receive every sigh of a frightened soul. For the one seeking refuge, heaven is always open, a place to unburden at any hour.

The Strong, however, must hold counsel with themselves. His heart must provide answers and accountability when his light begins to fade, threatening to cloud his perfection. The Strong knows he is lost—irretrievably lost—if the resonance of his soul, the harmony of perfection within the law, has vanished. He recognizes his own betrayal. This is the moment of his collapse, a collapse from which he seeks no rescue, for a life without loyalty, without honor, without duty, is meaningless.

Is it any wonder, then, that the half-hearted, the wavering, ask for a substitute for religion in the moment of decision and, not strong enough to achieve greatness, turn back to beg for blessings?

The Strong is anything but unfeeling. He simply does not wear his heart on his sleeve, for what fills his soul cannot be voiced as a prayer, exclamation, or lament to the blessing-giving heavens. The trials and sorrows of the soul are known to the Strong in his solitude, for even in the homeland of the Strong, clouds sometimes threaten to cover the sun. But the struggle that now begins within him is not one in the biblical sense.

"Lord, I will not let you go unless you bless me!"

This struggle is not for the comforting reconciliation with a stronger God but rather a battle with one's own weakness. The cries of fear, the tempting words of frailty, must be drowned out by the message of the will, which the Strong must revive from the deepest depths of his soul in his struggle with himself.

The Strong either breaks or emerges from the fight twice as steadfast and purified. This is the "blessing and grace" of this world—or perhaps the "Judgment Day" of the heart.

Thus, in the struggle for perfection—rising above chasms, constantly at risk of falling and shattering—the Strong grows into his homeland, which is the place of his humanity's activity, yet not a sanctuary for the vague concept of humanity. Humanity is already the sum, the collection of knowing individuals, while "humankind" remains merely a formal category. Here, too, the essential distinctions have been blurred by boundary-blurring weaklings.

Apostles of humanity have especially arisen under the emblem of apron and trowel, aiming to build Solomon's Temple from the hewn stones of all peoples and races. To "be a human," to "have human rights," has seemed the ultimate in this world.

The Strong has sent his message to the world: the highest purpose in this world is to have duty, because;

"Who stands in duty, stands in honor!"

True humanity emerges only where duty has lifted man beyond himself, enabling him to uphold loyalty and honor.

Only within this humanity are values born, values achieved through the purifying struggle of a knowing, lawful life. While the foundations may be placed in the child's cradle, humanity itself is never inherited. The foundations lie dormant within one's heritage, but they must be drawn out through education, self-discipline, vigilance, and continuous struggle.

Religions too easily offer those who are "halfway" a sweet veil of comfort, suggesting they may yet be "chosen" by God's grace, covering their pitiful nakedness.

Yet, by forging a homeland for their deeds and desires, the Strong open the gate to the future for all who one day will undertake the arduous journey from half-measures to completeness.

The more incorruptible, resolute, free, and uncompromising the first settlers of this homeland are, the greater will be the land they conquer through their labor. The Strong know that, while their battle is filled with pain and danger, their successors will have a less burdensome fight! They are the knights of freedom, conquering new land where a thriving people shall one day sow and reap for all eternity.

Their will is their sword, defiance their shield, lawfulness their armor: thus fight the knights of this time for their new homeland!

They have only one god above them: duty. Only one command binds them: honor. Only one goal remains fixed before them: the nation of this world, the Germanic Reich of the German Nation, as long as it stands real and as long as one Strong still fights for the homeland of this new reality.

The knights receive but one reward: the joyful, jubilant "Yes" of the heart, grateful to live and fight for completeness in lawfulness!

Amidst curses and blessings, undeterred by the praise of the half-hearted or the rage of the weak, the Strong strides forward to the homeland of this world, which has now become reality from the stars of longing.

He cares not for the snares set by hypocrites but for one thing alone: to bring the pure flame of his heart to his waiting brothers, heralding the dawn of freedom!

CHAPTER

6

THE MIGHTY HOMELAND!

Freedom's wings were once clipped when the Cross cast its shadow over the world. The vitality of life faded, and with it began the withering of all that is called the values of humanity: culture, art, society. Most deadly was that the soul was assigned a realm distant from life, a place far removed from the heart and blood.

It was madness to believe that one could capture a note and preserve it without the instrument that created it! To remove the soul from a human is to leave behind a ruin—what use is it to place the soul with God if, in the process, humanity dies? How could one's heart beat outside the body?

To rob a race of its soul is to hollow it out, to strip it of growth, turning it into something that quickly fades. The envoys of Yahweh pursued no other goal than to desoul this world. The trail of death they left behind reveals more of their intentions than their grand words could hide.

It took long for the exiled heroes to return to their homeland. But the day of their return marks the dawn of freedom's resurrection.

The new human rises in unity with the law, which fuses life and longing, vision and reality, into uncompromising action. The cage of the soul is shattered, and powerfully it stirs its wings for a new ascent.

Steadfast is the stride of the Strong, who reclaims his homeland. Steadfast are his thoughts. And steadfast is the sound of his voice.

He stands tall, realizing he has grown to the height of the stars, and the mundane world with its petty concerns and constraints fades into insignificance beneath him.

Steadfast is the stride of the Strong as he steps into his homeland.

Steadfast are his thoughts.

And steadfast is the sound of his voice.

He stands tall, perceiving he has grown to the height of the stars, while the trivial concerns and constraints of the everyday world sink beneath him into insignificance.

Where is God?

This is the cry that the everyday world hurls toward the heavens, hoping for an answer to the ultimate mystery of all things.

The Strong, alone in his solitude, turns to look for the God that the world imagines to be enthroned above the stars.

Long he looks, until he sees that nowhere in the endless expanse of stars is there a throne room of a God. Nowhere does he glimpse the shapes of angels and saints. Nowhere does he hear a pious *Hallelujah*.

But the more intently the Strong listens into infinity, the more clearly he hears the harmonious rhythm of a distant resonance, a sound of ultimate purity. This resonance is caused by the eternal rhythm that the Law has set within the universe.It is the rhythm of all life, all decay, all becoming anew: the rhythm of creation, into which flows all that lives and from which flows all that gives life. The Law, then, is the highest will to create, and so it acts within all that flows out and all that flows in.

Eternities are but seconds within the Law, and the universe is the vast body of creation, whose soul, heart, and blood, whose unity and ultimate reality is the will of the Law.

Greater than all gods, more eternal than their wonders, commandments, and decrees, is the will of the Law. It demands only action, not weakness. Thus, it lives within the Strong, while the Weak only experiences the illusion of reality, mirrored in his own imagination.

The more powerfully the rhythm of creation is revealed in a person, the more powerful, pure, and incorruptible will be his actions, his life, his vision, and his reality.

The Strong does not ask for a god's grace to be lifted like a child into his arms to see a play; he demands to stand as an adult, to understand!

Perfection, therefore, is the goal of true humanity.

Let the Weak climb to the tops of their church towers to seek their god from that tiny height; the Strong laughs at them.

His homeland needs no church towers! The homeland of the Strong is on the highest heights of this world, where the stars shine more clearly than in the lowlands, where the sky is clearer than over the valleys.

"Where is God?" chant the chorales from the valleys below. "What must I do to earn his grace?" echoes the tortured heart from the lowlands!

But the Strong opens his arms to embrace an entire world. His soul is at home in harmony; it sings the same note as that distant resonance.

There, no chatter of prayers, no humble hymns of repentance are heard: there is only the triumphant cry of freedom, the jubilation of life's true eternity.

Thus, the homeland of the Strong is a land of joy, the joy of imperishable strength.

In the Land of Eternal Strength, free humanity builds gathering places in the rhythm of its race that are mightier than churches and cathedrals: these are the sites of culture, constructed from the visions that pure blood calls forth from the depths of a heart devoted to creation and the knowledge of the Law. This culture, with its art that embraces the entirety of eternal life, is the joyful gratitude of humanity to the life-giving, strength-bestowing Law.

This art has the ultimate purpose of making the eyes of the Strong shine with the eternity of creative action. Each work of art thus becomes a victory song of freedom.

The victory songs of the Strong celebrate the virtue of humanity near to the stars: the highest duty to remain strong and to overcome all weakness, because weakness means death.

Whoever's strength falters at the highest heights, whose knees begin to tremble at the edges of the abyss, will shatter into the void. Yet it is not about preserving the individual; it is about safeguarding the spirit of the race, whose full song should resonate from thousands of jubilant hearts.

Nations are the strongest and, thus, the true masters of the Earth, whose song is the fullest and most life-affirming.

Mighty homeland, Germany, from whose heart rises the mountain!

Homeland Germany, you are the primal mother of the Strong, who has borne your sons to be guardians on the towers of freedom!

If there is a blessing of fate, it is to be of German blood!

The joyful message of duty, which the homeland of the strong imposes on its guardians, speaks of the relentlessness of perfect life that, for the sake of love, demands hardness. Therefore, the strong forge their hearts in the fire of longing for perfection.

Perfect is the one who can blend the sound of their complete personality into the harmony of the Law without the slightest discord.

This is the beauty of perfection: it means a life of wakefulness, a life without numbness.

Truth, with its harsh face full of infinite knowledge, is beautiful; it is, for the strong, the elixir of eternal youth. But for the weak, it becomes deadly poison.

To have a homeland means to say "yes" to all the consequences and demands of knowledge and will, to experience the vitality of life in duty.

The sacred ground of the homeland is truth soaked with the blood of the best.

The iron will that tills this soil, the seed of knowledge planted within it, and the ripening fruit of insight that springs forth—all of this combines to become the bread of true life in this world.

This bread is the nourishment for the soul of the strong.

What is the manna of heaven compared to this bread?

The strong have a duty to be "good."

Their goodness is directed toward the preservation and care of life. This goodness is defined by the will to uphold the law.

The will to uphold the law is focused on eternal becoming, on a conscious growth toward unity with creation—a deliberate act of creation in reality for eternity.

Mighty homeland, Germany! Homeland of the strong!

As twilight surrounded the earth, the mountain began to glow at midnight.

A new earth cast its first shadow.

The old gods have long been buried, with heavy stones laid over their graves.

When Asgard fell, heaven sought to become a refuge for the weak and a triumph for those against life.

Heaven, too, has long passed.

A third rose up when the weak believed the end of all days had come: the homeland of the strong!

And with this homeland of the strong, a new era begins on this ancient, ever-renewing earth.

The joy of this new era does not lie in some dreamy distant bliss but in the jubilant fulfillment of duty, to which one is called according to the order of their worth.

It is not redeemed angels who sing the song of praise in this creation, but perfected humans, letting their hearts resonate in the jubilant rhythm of their fulfilled lives.

There is only one place of damnation: to be far from the heart of this homeland!

BROTHERS OF FATE

POETRY

KURT EGGERS

Brothers of Fate...

... Darkness veils the horror.

Only the brothers of fate gaze
With steadfast hearts into the night.

Lonely, they march into battle,
For the realm, the new, the free,
To build up the future.

Thrones of gods, corpses of gods
Must yield to a future
That knows nothing but strong hearts.

Gold, possessions, and jewels,
Are mere illusion, deceit, and lies,

When fate demands true values!
Masks are torn down by fate.

Under their godly masks,
Beneath many golden trinkets,
You see senseless old men tremble,
As the wind flutters their scraps.

Upon the ruins of that yesterday
You finally, finally see again,
Marching with steady steps,
Into distant horizons,
Our brothers of fate stride.

Theirs will be the land,
And earth.

That the dawn may finally come,
They head towards the sunrise,
Over corpses, over ruins,
They must lay the beams
That will support the structure of the future.

Without lament,
Without complaints,
They are themselves stone and mortar,
Ax and chisel,
Hammer and anvil.

Above the wailing of old Gods
Rises the battle cry
Of young people
Who have found themselves,
Since fate has repeatedly
Hurled hailstones over fields,
War flags over nations,
Death that laid peoples low.

Brothers of fate
Are we.

Stronger, greater, truer, more real than the gods,
Whom we cast down into the dust!

www.ingramcontent.com/pod-product-compliance
Lightning Source LLC
Chambersburg PA
CBHW041933260326
41914CB00010B/1280